The
Complete Player

The Complete Player

THE PSYCHOLOGY OF WINNING HOCKEY

Dr. Saul L. Miller

Published in 2001 by
Stoddart Publishing Co. Limited
895 Don Mills Road, 400-2 Park Centre, Toronto, Canada M3C 1W3
PMB 128, 4500 Witmer Estates, Niagara Falls, New York 14305-1386

www.stoddartpub.com

To order Stoddart books please contact General Distribution Services
In Canada Tel. (416) 213-1919   Fax (416) 213-1917
Email cservice@genpub.com
In the United States
Toll-free tel. 1-800-805-1083 Toll-free fax 1-800-481-6207
Email gdsinc@genpub.com

10 9 8 7 6 5 4 3 2

National Library of Canada Cataloguing in Publication Data
Miller, Saul, 1942–
The complete player: the psychology of winning hockey

ISBN 0-7737-6221-3

1. Hockey — Psychological aspects.   2. Hockey — Training.   I. Title.
GV848.3.M54 2001   796.962′01′9   C2001-901813-4

Publisher Cataloging in Publication Data (U.S.)
Miller, Saul.
The complete player: the psychology of winning hockey / Saul Miller. —
1st pbk. ed.
[256] p. : cm.

ISBN 0-7737-6221-3 (pbk.)

1. Hockey players — Training of.   2. Hockey — Training. I. Title.
796.962   21   2002   CIP GV848.3.M55

Cover Design: The Bang
Text Design: Kinetics Design & Illustration

THE CANADA COUNCIL | LE CONSEIL DES ARTS
FOR THE ARTS | DU CANADA
SINCE 1957 | DEPUIS 1957

We acknowledge for their financial support of our publishing program the Canada Council, the Ontario Arts Council, and the Government of Canada through the Book Publishing Industry Development Program (BPIDP).

Printed and bound in Canada

I would like to dedicate this book to the guys I first played hockey with on the ice and snow at Ponsard Park in Montreal. To Marty, Ax, Morty, Brian, Kess, Johnny Joe, Louie, and Skippy; to Gerry Snyder, who organized hockey in our neighborhood; and to the NHLers who inspired us: Maurice "Rocket" Richard, Teeder Kennedy, Henri "the Pocket Rocket" Richard, Doug Harvey, Gordie Howe, Ted Lindsay, Alex Delvecchio, Walter "Turk" Broda, Jacques Plante, Jean Beliveau, Bernie "Boom Boom" Geoffrion, Andy Bathgate, Terry Sawchuk, Lorne "Gump" Worsley, Tim Horton, and to Roger Neilson, a dedicated hockey man, a successful and innovative coach, and a kind and caring fellow.

Contents

Preface

The object of hockey is relatively simple: put the puck in your opponents' goal and keep them from putting it in yours. At the end of an hour of play, the team that has scored the most goals wins.

Beyond that simple aim, however, hockey is a fast-paced game of skill, one that requires highly developed abilities to skate, read the play, and react quickly. You must also be able to control the puck, which means that players devote countless hours to the building up of their stickhandling, passing, and shooting skills.

Hockey can be an intense, physically aggressive, and sometimes violent game. Body-checking, stick-checking, shot-blocking, and fighting are all part of a sport that demands mobility, toughness, strength, and courage.

Finally, hockey is a team game. It requires that players learn to work together and adapt their skills to the team's system and game plan.

In preparing athletes to play hockey, most coaches emphasize the physical and technical aspects of the game. Drills stress skating, conditioning, puck control, passing, and shooting. But the mental aspect of hockey has been relatively neglected. *The Complete Player* aims to address this training imbalance, both by describing the mental training techniques that have proven successful among a wide range of elite hockey players and by sharing many of those players' insights into the game.

Sport psychology can be a valuable coaching resource. Most players who consult with me want to play well. Usually, they are seeking improvement in some aspect of their game — they want to improve their scoring, play better defensively, or in the case of goaltenders, to improve their ability to stop the puck. Sometimes they are playing well but they feel anxious. Or they're "squeezing" the stick — the more they try, the less effective they seem to be. Some want to learn how to be more focused, prepare better, develop better mental discipline, or feel more confident. Others have been injured and are looking for something to help them to return to form. Still others are struggling to adapt to a system or to get along with a coach. Finally, there are those who consult with me because they are having trouble getting "up" for games, perhaps because they are coping with a multitude of distractions on and off the ice.

As a sport psychologist I have worked with hockey players for almost 20 years, both at the NHL and developmental levels. I've observed that there are three basics to winning the mental game of hockey:

Right focus. Put simply, knowing what you want to do on the ice, staying tuned in, and working to make that happen.

Right feeling. By this I mean creating and maintaining feelings that will help you play your best. For some that means feeling energized and "up"; others prefer to be calm, confident, composed, and centered. All players should avoid being distracted by feelings like fear, anger, pain, or fatigue.

Right attitude. A winning hockey attitude is one with the motivation, commitment, and love of the game to persevere and excel.

In this book I will share observations and mental training techniques I have used to help people play and coach winning hockey. The examples that will be presented are all based on real players and real on-ice experiences. To maintain the confidentiality of clients past and present, I have changed the identity and names of some of the players and coaches described in the examples.

The techniques described in this book are applicable to all players regardless of sex. As most of my clients have been male, for the sake of simplicity I will use the male singular pronoun when referring to players throughout the book.

Acknowledgments

I wish to thank the following individuals who contributed to my experience of the game and to the writing of this book. To my literary agent, Robert Mackwood; the team at Stoddart, Angel Guerra, Jim Gifford, Lloyd Davis, Ron Wight; and Dr. Laara Maxwell, Dave Hammond, Martin Wright, and Garfield Miller for editorial comments and suggestions.

Thanks also to coaches Scotty Bowman, Marc Crawford, Gary Davidson, Glen Hanlon, Mark Holick, Mike Keenan, Rick Lanz, Jack McIlhargey, Andy Moog, Mike Murphy, Harry Neale, Roger Neilson, Pat Quinn, Doug Risebrough, Larry Robinson, Duane Sutter, Stan Smyl, Bob Tunstead, and Barry Wolfe; scouts Bart Brady, John Chapman, Ron Delorme, Frank Fay, and Mike Penny; trainers and doctors Larry Ashley, Mike Burnstein, Pete Demers, Peter Twist, and Ross Davidson; and, most especially, the players — both those I've worked with over the years, and those who were kind enough to assist me on this project: Adrian Aucoin, Derek Bekar, Ken Berry,

Donald Brashear, Pavel Bure, Jim Fox, Garry Galley, Scott Gomez, Anders Hakansson, Mark Hardy, Bret Hedican, Darby Hendrickson, Jamie Huscroft, Bob Janecyk, Ed Jovanovski, Paul Kariya, Steve Kariya, Trent Klatt, Grant Ledyard, Morris Lukowich, Kevin McCarthy, Dave Mackey, Brad May, Rollie Melanson, Scott Mellanby, Mark Messier, Alfie Michaud, Alexander Mogilny, Bill Muckalt, Markus Naslund, Jim Nill, Mattias Ohlund, Bobby Orr, Chuck Ottewell, Larry Playfair, Chris Pronger, Craig Redmond, Luc Robitaille, Cliff Ronning, Dave Scatchard, Corey Schwab, Jeff Sharples, Billy Smith, Doug Smith, Stan Smyl, Garth Snow, Brent Sopel, Steve Staios, Dave Taylor, John Vanbiesbrouck, Joe Vandermeer, Kevin Weekes, Dave "Tiger" Williams, Joel Williams, and Mitch Wolfe, plus the players of the Syracuse Crunch of the American Hockey League, the Surrey Eagles, Langley Hornets, and Langley Thunder of the British Columbia Hockey League, the Tri-City Americans of the Western Hockey League, and the Kelowna Minor Hockey Association.

Introduction

Why do some players score lots of goals while others with seemingly equal skills rarely score at all? How is it that some players are able to stay focused while others are easily distracted by the pressure and violence of the game? What is the best way to prepare for a game?

Is there something a player can say to himself to play better? How do I get out of a slump? How do players keep themselves sharp and shift-ready despite sitting on the bench for long periods of time? How do players get "up" for the game shift after shift, night after night, throughout a long hockey season?

How can players use visualization and imagery to be more effective? Why do defensemen use visualization more than forwards? How can I increase my confidence and sense of pride? What can I do to become mentally tougher?

How can I make recovering from an injury a positive experience?

We will explore all of these issues and provide sport psychology training suggestions to help you become a more complete player. This is not just a book, it's a training camp.

I have set up this book so that it mirrors my standard method of consulting with a player. The first five chapters are presented as if I am working with a player who has come to see me to improve his on-ice performance. I usually begin by listening to a player describe his game, his interests, and his concerns; then I discuss some basic principles about how the mind works and the importance of mind-body balance in creating the right performance state for hockey. This is covered in Chapter 1.

In Chapter 2 I discuss "right feelings" and how players can use breathing to release excessive tension and calm down — or to energize and pump up.

Chapters 3 and 4 explore focus, both in regard to power thoughts (Chapter 3) and high-performance imagery (Chapter 4).

In Chapter 5 I discuss a winning attitude. Specifically, I look at four elements of winning: commitment, confidence, identity, and love of the game. Examples and suggestions describe what a player (or coach) can do to bring these forces more into play.

Chapter 6 sheds some light on the mental qualities that NHL scouts and coaches look for in players and concludes with a discussion of "mental toughness."

Chapter 7 looks at individual differences and offers some suggestions as to how players with differing personality styles can prepare to maximize performance.

As I've already mentioned, hockey is a team game, and team play is essential to team success. In Chapter 8 I discuss teamwork and the keys to becoming a team player.

I would recommend that anyone who wants to use the book as a training camp read through the entire book first, then go back and work on the chapters that interest them most. Chapters 1 through 8 contain homework assignments; if your interest is to improve your game, then I recommend doing the assignments at the end of each chapter.

Chapters 9, 10, and 11 discuss scoring, playing defense, and tending goal, and contain insights from many experienced NHL players. Wherever possible, I have tried to relate their comments and the demands of their position to the training suggestions presented earlier.

Chapter 9 focuses on scoring and includes training suggestions from NHL scorers, including Mark Messier, Pavel Bure, Paul Kariya, and Cliff Ronning.

Chapter 10 focuses on playing defense and includes tips from such present and former NHLers as Mattias Ohlund, Larry Robinson, Garry Galley, and Chris Pronger, as well as checkers like Bob Gainey, Brad May, and Tiger Williams.

Chapter 11 focuses on applying "hockey psyche" training to the unique challenges of playing goal. The chapter includes comments and advice from experienced NHL goalies such as John Vanbiesbrouck, Garth Snow, Glen Hanlon, and Andy Moog.

Because hockey is a physically aggressive game, Chapter 12 provides some mental training tips on recovering from hockey injuries and recharging for future games. The chapter concludes with a look at lifestyle choices that support consistent, high-level on-ice performance.

Finally, Chapter 13 discusses growing talent and hockey values.

⎯⎯○

While writing this book I spoke with many players, coaches, and scouts, all of whom shared their experiences and insights about preparation, feeling, focus, and a winning attitude. Two things are clear from our discussions. First of all, people are different — there is no one prescription or technique that fits all. Second, whether you are a player or coach, whether you are interested in developing individual skills or winning teams, there's a two-step process that people seem to follow to improve their game. They *assess* and *adjust*.

First, be aware and assess yourself. Who am I? (Or, in the case of a team, Who are we?) What's the situation? What has to be done for me/us to improve and succeed? Then, adjust your technique or training (to improve). When you're done, reassess. Development in hockey — and in life — is a continuous process. Throughout the book, whether we are discussing emotional control, self-talk, imagery, or attitude, whether it's about playing forward, defense, or goal, the way to improve your play is to be aware of your needs and circumstances, make the appropriate adjustment, then reassess your performance. Your development as a complete player is not only about working on your strengths; it is directly proportional to how honestly you evaluate your abilities and your willingness to put in the necessary effort on those parts of your game that you need to improve.

Rick's Story

Rick Lanz was a junior all-star with the Oshawa Generals of the Ontario Hockey League who was selected by the Vancouver Canucks in the first round of the NHL Entry Draft. At the age of 19 he made his debut with the Canucks. "I had experienced a lot of pressure in junior hockey, but somehow I managed to survive and play well," he says. "When the Canucks drafted me I don't think I was prepared for the intensity and pressure of the NHL." Much is expected of first-round draft picks, and Rick felt a tremendous obligation to play well every night. Off the ice, there were many distractions: the travel, the attention from the press and fans, and the long NHL schedule.

Rick was the kind of player who would worry about his performance. He hadn't yet learned to focus his energies, control his emotions, and manage his mind. "I know now that's the realm of sport psychology," he says, "but at that time I'd had no exposure to it.

"I remember scoring a goal and getting two assists in my very first game, being selected first star, and being heralded as the next Bobby Orr. I really wanted to meet everyone's expectations.

"I played fairly well. I made some mistakes, but I was learning the ropes. One thing I noticed was that I sometimes got caught up in the distractions. I would come to the rink and try and get ready for the game and then realize it wasn't enough. I had to start thinking about things and getting myself ready to play much earlier, way before the game began."

About halfway through his second season, Rick seriously injured his knee and had to undergo major surgery. Not only was he devastated by the injury and uncertain whether he would ever return to top form, but he missed out completely on the Canucks' improbable run all the way to the 1982 Stanley Cup finals.

"After the season and a whole lot of rehab, the team's orthopedic surgeon sent me to the Canucks' sport psychologist. He said it was to help me regain my confidence. To be frank, I needed some help. That's when I met Dr. Saul Miller."

As we worked together, Rick began to get excited about playing again. In 1983–84 he set a Canucks record for power-play goals by a defenseman that stood for 15 years, and was named the team's best defenseman. "I think a big reason for my success was that I was a more complete player," he says. "I now had some good techniques that helped me prepare, focus, stay calm, and tune out the distractions and negativity. I was able to enjoy the game more.

"I continued to apply all the techniques diligently for several years. They were my best years in the NHL. Then I stopped using them. It's a funny thing. Success sometimes makes people take things for granted. In retrospect I realize that as I got away from my mental training my performance declined. I played for 10 more years for a variety of coaches — and through some serious injuries — and I can honestly say that when I really worked on the mental game was when I played best."

Chapter 1

Operating Your Mental TV

Success in hockey — and success in life — is about learning to manage your mind. By managing the mind effectively, I mean setting clear, challenging goals; creating empowering feelings; defining your specific on-ice tasks; running "power" thoughts and images; tuning out negativity and distraction; and nurturing a positive, winning attitude.

It's the beginning of training camp — a new season is about to begin. Standing before me are 40 prospective NHLers. The head coach has just addressed the rookies, telling them about the excellent opportunity that training camp offers. Indeed, ever since they were kids, many of these young athletes have been dreaming of going to an NHL camp and making the team.

"Some of you will make the team this year," the coach has said. "Some of you will play in the NHL in the next few years. Some of you will learn things in this camp that you will take with you and that will help you to be better players and better people."

The coach goes on to lay out the rules and regulations of training camp, then introduces me, the team's sport psychologist. As I get up to speak I recognize a mix of curiosity, interest, and uncertainty on the players' faces. I pick up where the coach left off, talking about opportunity.

"This camp is an opportunity," I tell them. "And I believe the best way to manage an opportunity is by managing your mind." I underline the importance of two things that will help them to play well.

The first is to maintain a positive and productive focus throughout the camp. For most of them, the camp will represent a new, pressure-filled experience. There are many things they may be thinking about, but I encourage them to focus their thinking on the positive — especially where it applies to what they want to do on the ice.

I tell them not to worry about what the coach is thinking. "Don't waste your time and energy wondering, 'Why did he put me on this line and not on that line?' Don't worry whether he noticed what you did or didn't do on the last shift. Don't dwell on a poor play or a poor shift. You get more of what you think about, so keep focused on the positives."

I tell them to concentrate on the things that got them here, things like moving their feet, passing tape to tape, playing the body, finishing their checks, shooting accurately, and working hard.

The second thing I tell the group is that they need to control their feelings. I explain a little bit about how feelings affect thinking, and how breathing can be an important way of controlling those emotions that can interfere with performance. "Just taking a breath can help you to feel more calm and control feelings like fear and anger that pop up." Then I tell them how anxious feelings may cause them to squeeze the stick, or wonder whether they should or shouldn't fight. And how common these feelings are at training camp, when players want so badly to impress the coach.

I keep my comments brief because I know that now is not the

time for a detailed explanation or for any in-depth mental training. These young men want to get on the ice and play hockey. They are motivated to excel, to be great. They want to show what they can do. I will consult with them in greater depth later on in the camp and during the season.

Within the week, I will consult with several rookies individually. One of them, Ken, is a young defenseman who had an excellent training camp and exhibition season last year. He felt he should have made the NHL team, but instead he spent the season in the American Hockey League, where he played very well.

I begin by asking Ken how things are going. He replies that he's feeling good, but acknowledges that he's nervous. He really wants to make a good impression. He wonders if there is something I can do to help him play with more confidence so he can have an even better camp than he did last year.

I observe that wanting to do well is admirable, but unchanneled emotion often leads a player to try too hard, which can be a hindrance. I ask Ken: "If you were a coach looking at a young prospect, what could he do that would impress you and indicate that he is ready to be on your NHL team?"

"Play with confidence," he replies.

"Okay, and how would you go about doing that?" I ask. "What specific things could you do on the ice that would give you a sense of confidence?"

"Well, I would skate well, move the puck well, make good passes, finish my checks, and be strong in clearing the front of our net."

"Can you do these things at this level?"

"Absolutely," Ken replies.

I point out that it's important to have a clear, positive idea of what to do on the ice — and it sounds to me like he does. With that in mind, confidence comes from two places: having the right feelings — that is, believing in your ability to do the right things on the ice, and then actually doing them. One thing Ken can do to build confidence is to visualize himself making the plays he has just described.

We spend some time doing relaxation and visualization exercises.

Ken goes on to have a good camp and by the end of November is playing a regular shift on the NHL club.

How much of the game is mental? A good question, and one I discussed with veteran NHL coach Roger Neilson. Roger told me that, when he was with the Philadelphia Flyers, the team's sport psychologist put that very question to the players at a team meeting. "Raise your hand when I get to the percentage you think is the best answer," he told them.

According to Roger, no one raised his hand at 30 percent, or even 40 or 50 percent. A few hands were raised at 60 percent and a few more at 70, but most of the players raised their hands at 80 percent. The question could easily be debated endlessly; what most athletes and coaches would agree on is that, given a certain level of physical ability, success in sports is mostly "mental." It relies on focus, determination, and emotional control, and it's the result of mind and body working well together.

Excellence in any sport is the result of the successful integration of physical, technical, and mental factors. Curiously, however, in most sports a disproportionate focus is placed on the physical and technical aspects of training, while mental training is relatively ignored. It's no less true in hockey.

I asked Doug Risebrough, a former NHL player and coach who is now the general manager of an NHL expansion team, the Minnesota Wild, how he began the process of building a winner. "First," he said, "select people of character. Choose guys who are winners, who want to win, and who are willing to work together to make that happen." Doug added that resiliency is a key quality that goes hand in hand with being a winner. He also cited the following traits: having a team goal and the ability to stay positive, focused, and keep working hard, no matter what happens.

Are positivity, focus, and resiliency qualities that can be learned or "coached"?

I think so.

Stimulus-Response

Psychology is the study of behavior. One way of studying behavior is to break it down into stimulus and response units. A *stimulus* is something that we perceive — it can be something we see, hear, or think. A *response* is a way of reacting to what we perceive. In sport we are constantly surrounded by and bombarded with thousands of stimuli. To be effective in hockey, a player must be selective and focus on specific stimuli or cues. That's what we mean when we say make "good reads." Then he must respond to these stimuli in specific, effective ways. The whole process is instantaneous. For example, the defenseman, while skating and watching the puck, reads a two-on-one situation — a complex stimulus situation — and responds by positioning himself to take away the pass. The goalie reads the same stimulus situation and responds by playing the shooter — and reacting to the movement of the puck.

Thinking can be both a stimulus and a response. A thought can stimulate action, yet also be a response to something we have perceived. For example, a player can think about his role and responsibility — "First man in on the forecheck takes the body" — which is a stimulus for action, and respond by attacking the defenseman with the puck. Or, he can think of his commitment to playing with discipline on each and every shift (which is a stimulus) and respond by staying with his check rather than chasing the puck.

Now consider how thinking can also be a response. After a good shift, a player can say something to himself like, "Good work. That's me: that's how I'm capable of playing," which is a thinking response that builds confidence. After a poor shift where he left his man open in front of the net, a player can respond by thinking, "I can do better than that. That's not me. I always stay between my man and the net." Similarly, a player can read external (what's happening on the ice) or internal stimuli (feelings like fatigue and pain) and adjust his game accordingly. Going into his third game in four nights, Joe, a tough rushing defenseman who played more than 25 minutes a game, was feeling sore and tired. Reading these feelings (internal stimuli), he adjusted and simplified his game a little. While still playing hard, he rushed less and focused more on his defensive responsibilities.

The way you manage your thinking and feeling (your mind) is basic to how you perform. It's up to you. Improving your game begins with taking responsibility for managing your mind.

Three Principles for Managing Your Mind

I believe there are three key operating principles for managing the mind effectively.

The first idea or principle is that the mind is like a TV set. It's always on, thinking thoughts, running images, and creating feelings. What's important to understand is that you control the channel changer on that mental TV. If what you're watching

doesn't give you power or doesn't feel good to you, then change the channel. My job as a sport psychologist is to show you two things: how to change channels on your mental TV and how to develop better quality programs to tune in to.

The second principle of effective performance is that you get more of what you think about. There is a mental phenomenon called "lateral inhibition" — whatever stimulus we focus on becomes magnified in our perceptual field, while all other stimuli are downplayed. If you are worried and focus on thoughts and feelings that cause you anxiety (for instance, failure, embarrassment, pain, or disappointment), these thoughts and this reality will become magnified in your mind. Thinking thoughts like "We're going to blow this lead," "This guy is impossible to check," "How am I supposed to play with these guys as my linemates?" or "I can't put the puck in the net" all increase the likelihood of a negative performance.

Many players are negative thinkers. At a meeting of a midget

AAA team I asked a 16-year-old player how many shots he took in a game. He thought for a moment and said, "Five or six." Then he added, "And I'll probably miss the net on all of them." With thinking like that, he's probably right.

You may say, "Well, he's just a kid," but according to Larry Robinson, a perennial NHL all-star defenseman who is now a successful NHL head coach, the pros are just as hard on themselves. "Too many guys [in the NHL] come off the ice and dwell on their mistakes," he says. "There's not enough focusing on the positive aspect of the game."

On the other hand, if you concentrate on the things you want to make happen on the ice, you will increase the chance of these things happening. Positive results will follow.

It's important to think positive and to put positive "power" programs on your mental TV. Sounds simple, yet very few people are able to stay tuned in to positive thoughts and feelings all the time. Experts tell us that we think 50,000 to 60,000 thoughts a day. And for most people, more than 80 percent of the thoughts they have are negative or self-critical. Which brings us to our third principle.

That is that our feelings affect our thoughts, and our thoughts affect our feelings. This explains why we sometimes get stuck on the negatives even though we know we should think positively. It boils down to the way we're "wired" as human beings, the way our nervous systems work. Every time we have a feeling, a thought automatically goes with it. If the feelings you are experiencing are fear, pain, or uncertainty, the thoughts you think will tend to be stress-inducing and limiting. On the other hand, if you are feeling strong, energetic, and in control, your thoughts will be more positive and your confidence will grow.

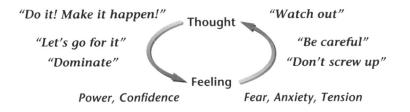

The feelings that most frequently limit hockey players have to do with fear, anger, frustration, fatigue, and pain. Here are some examples of how negative feelings can affect thinking.

Feeling		Thought
Fear (of failure)	⟹	"Don't make another mistake," "Don't screw up"
Fear (of injury)	⟹	"Watch out," "Be careful"
Anger	⟹	"I'm going to get him!"
Frustration	⟹	"Something's wrong," "It's not happening"
	⟹	"There's no way," "What's the use?"
Fatigue	⟹	"I'm beat," "Not now, maybe later"
Pain	⟹	"Be careful," "Watch out"

Negative, limited feelings can produce negative, limited thinking, which in turn feeds back to create a negative loop that can become a trap. That's what a "slump" is all about: negative feelings — usually anxiety — feeding and producing negative thoughts that create more negative feelings.

Lou was a 30-goal-a-year scorer in the NHL. During those high-performance years he went to the net with confidence and abandon. He felt strong, fast, and self-assured and he just went for it. Then something unfortunate happened to him. As he drove to the net on a scoring chance he was slashed across the face. The slash cut him badly and broke his jaw. After the injury his feelings and his focus changed. He noticed he was tentative about going to the net. Instead of thinking, "I'll score," he began to think, "Watch out." He was looking to avoid the check as often as he was trying to put the puck in the net. His goal production dropped dramatically and his career faltered.

Lou's scoring touch recovered as a direct result of his becoming a better mental manager and learning to change the channel on limiting feelings of fear — and the thoughts that go with fear — and replacing them with feelings and thoughts of power and impact.

Excellence in hockey, as in any sport, is a function of mind and body working together effectively. It's about smooth, coordinated function between thought and action. Excessive tension and fearful or negative thoughts cause a separation or disintegration of mind and body that limits on-ice performance.

The question is, how can we integrate mind and body and thus reduce these limiting, negative thoughts and feelings? Learning how to do that is key to operating your mental TV efficiently and playing winning hockey. Understanding how to create powerful feelings and positive productive thoughts will enable you to create a state in which you can play at your best.

Your state is what you bring to any on-ice situation, whether it's in a game or a practice. And you are responsible for your state. Most people think the word "responsible" means that if you screw up, make a mistake, you're in for trouble. Actually, the word responsible means *response-able*. You are response-able for managing your mental TV. By that I mean you are response-able for creating the feelings and focus that will help you to excel on the ice.

The complete player takes response-ability for managing his mind in order to be the best he can be. Two basic mental training tips that can help you manage your feelings and focus are training and reminding yourself to:

1. have a clear focus, and keep it simple; and
2. use your breathing to create right feelings and to change channels on your mental TV.

Do both, and you will play and stay strong and smooth.

Right Focus

Clear focus begins with having clear goals. Goals help us direct our energy. I recommend that you set several types of goals, then write them down, say them out loud, and repeat them to yourself.

Set long-term or career goals. Some bantam-age players I work with, who are 14 and 15 years old, set personal "career" goals to play collegiate, junior, and even professional hockey. It helps to have a perspective that addresses why you play and where you want to go. You may set a goal be to be the best player you can be, to make an elite team — or simply to enjoy the game.

Set goals for the season. Define what you want to achieve in terms of scoring, plus/minus, and team play. Then determine what you must do in terms of conditioning, skill development, and team play to make these goals a reality.

Set immediate goals for your next practice and game. For example, you may set a goal in practice to work on defending one on one, improving your shot from the point, or perfecting your skating. Setting practice goals and then doing the work is a good way to enhance skill development.

Last but not least, **set team goals**. Hockey is a team game. Team successes are paramount to a successful and enjoyable season. I am referring to both small and large team successes.

Of course, goal setting is just the beginning. What's essential is that you realize what you have to do to accomplish your goals — then follow through. Once you've defined the basics, the "ABCs," of what you want to do on the ice, it's time to do what's necessary in terms of conditioning, skill development, "right focus," and hard work to execute those basics.

Being the complete player is about having a clear direction, working hard, and following through. It's also about having a winning attitude. It's about being committed, confident, mentally tough or resilient, and having a passion for the game.

Right Feelings

Winning hockey is about managing your feelings. Remember, our feelings affect our thoughts, and our thoughts affect our feelings. You can't maintain "right focus" without managing feelings of fear, anger, pain, and fatigue. As I said earlier, you're the boss when it comes to how you feel, think, and act. You are response-able. Run positive programs on your mental TV and you will get more of what you think about.

Matt, an NHL all-star, told me a wonderful story of something that happened to him early in his career before he achieved star status. Matt was playing for a coach who showed little faith in his ability, who didn't play him much, and who treated him poorly. "The coach upset me so much that I couldn't even look at his face in the dressing room," Matt said. "Whenever he walked into the room I had to look away." In the off-season as Matt worked hard preparing for the next season, he kept wondering and worrying how he was going to deal with this non-supportive coach whom he perceived as a huge negative obstacle for him in his hockey career.

Matt is a religious person with a strong faith. While participating in a Christian hockey camp during the summer he was asked about his relationship with his coach. Matt couldn't lie. "I mentioned that this was one area of my game where I had a problem. Then, I went to talk about other things. Afterwards one of the parents came up to me. She said, 'I don't know you. But you seem to have a real problem with your coach. My suggestion is that you pray for him. It can change everything.'"

Matt said, "I remember thinking, the way that coach has treated me and with my bad feelings for him, it would be very difficult for me to pray for him." However, Matt was desperate for things to change so he followed the hockey mom's advice and began to pray for the coach. He said he prayed for the coach every day.

"It was interesting," Matt said. "After a little while my feelings for the coach began to change. By the time the next season began the frustration and anger I had with the man had disappeared. At the start of the season the coach didn't play me very much. He sat me for half the team's exhibition games. But it didn't bother me. I felt fine." Whenever he had a chance Matt played well. Eventually, he was rewarded with more ice time. Again, relaxed and positive, he played better and better. Because of injuries to other players Matt was moved to the first line and went on to have a career year. The following year Matt was an NHL scoring leader and was acknowledged as one of the best players in the game.

The key for Matt was taking responsibility for his situation and changing his thinking and feelings from anger, frustration, and negativity to tolerance and positivity. Reflecting on the experience he said, "You can't play well when you're uptight, frustrated, and negative. You've got to find a way to focus on the positive. Prayer made the difference for me."

Not many hockey people would be willing to pray for those who upset them and treat them poorly. A more common response is anger, which perpetuates the existing feelings of dis-ease. Indeed, shortly after I heard Matt's story, a minor hockey coach called to say he was having a real problem with some of the parents of the boys he coached. He mentioned one father in particular who was upset that the coach wasn't giving his 14-year-old son the star treatment he felt his son deserved. I knew the coach to be a fair and capable person who put in a great deal of time and effort to provide his players with a very good hockey program. I mentioned the story Matt had told me and suggested that perhaps he should pray for the parent. He said, "Pray for that jerk? You've got to be kidding."

Matt's story highlights several of the keys to a winning mind that we outlined earlier. First, the mind is like a TV. (If you don't like what you think or feel, it's up to you to change the channel. You are response-able to change what's happening to you.) Second, you get more of what you think about. (Focus on how bad something or someone is and things are likely to get worse. Find a way to focus on something positive and empowering and things are more likely to move in a positive direction.) Third, your feelings affect your thinking. (Tense, angry, frustrated feelings usually lead to negative thinking, poor performance, and more negative feelings.) Lastly, attitude is a matter of choice. If you are confronted by a challenging, difficult situation, you always have a choice; either you use it or it'll use you.

Matt was a positive person. He chose to take responsibility, change his focus and his feelings, and "use" what was a very difficult situation for him. It paid off. It usually does.

I asked Stan Smyl, the Vancouver Canucks' all-time scoring leader and now a successful coach, what he found useful about the sport psychology work we did together when he was a player. Stan said, "I think it helps you to be more in control. It helps you to control your emotions as you prepare for games and even during a game. That's important so you don't get too wound up and so you can think clearly and positively."

I agree with Stan's assessment. Winning hockey is about tuning in to winning programs. It's about creating "right feelings" and "right focus." We'll begin our training with "right feelings" in Chapter 2.

HOMEWORK ⇒

There is one homework assignment for Chapter 1.

Assignment 1 ⇒

Set your goals. As you begin reading this book, take the time to reflect on why you play hockey. What motivates you? What do you want to accomplish or achieve? I think it's very important to ask yourself these questions. The goals we set in hockey — and in life — come from our wants and desires. What do you want from the game?

_____

_____

Goals are about energy. They are desire channeled into direction. Your goals are a force you can use to energize your work habits, color your self-talk and imagery, and strengthen your attitude and team play. Research has shown that setting goals increases success.

Take a few minutes to answer the following questions:

Why do you play hockey?

Because I love the game

What do you want to achieve?

I want to show people my real potential as a hockey → no one has seen it yet _player_

Do you have a long-term hockey goal (or goals)? A career goal?

Improve constantly and always play at the highest level that I am capable of

What is your goal for the season?

Explosion → more speed to my game & scoring

To achieve your season goals, you will have to work on your conditioning, skills, and ability to read the play and react. List your fitness goals for the season (for example, improvement in strength, aerobic capacity, etc.).

improvement in strength (especially explosion), keeping in shape

List your skill goals for the season (improvement in skating, passing, shooting, checking).

improvement all-around

List your mental strength goals for the season (improvement in on-ice focus, pregame preparation, emotional control).

Being able to control my emotions, being able to visualize, mental toughness

List your team-play goals for the season (improvement in discipline, toughness, hard work, leadership).

be the leader I always am, always encourage my teammates, be a leader and show it off by how hard u work.

List a challenging and satisfying goal for your team to achieve this season.

Make playoffs - start winning games!

Goals direct our energy. If you are clear that your goal is to be the best player you can be, then it's helpful to define a purpose or goal for each practice and game — something specific that you will work to improve. If you are unclear about something specific that you want improve on, consult with your coach.

Select a goal for your next practice.
See net, shoot & score (train myself to do this)

Select a goal for your next game.
See net, shoot & score (after imagining it & practicing it, do it)

Goals are a driving force. They are a way of putting desire to work. To make your goal a reality, get in touch with what you want to do and write it down. Read it, say it, and repeat it to yourself. Understand what you will have to work on to realize that goal — whether it's improving your skating, foot speed, strength, stick skills, or ability to read the game — then start to work, and persevere, to make it happen.

Doing the homework assignments is an important part of developing a winning hockey psyche. Make the effort to explore your goals now, then revisit them after reading the book, at the start of a new season, and at regular intervals throughout the season.

Chapter 2

Right Feelings: Attack and Smooth

Hockey is an emotional game. If you're scoring and winning, you feel good. If you've been slashed, you get angry. If you lose, you become embarrassed. If you miss the net, you get down on yourself. If you're uncertain, you feel anxious; if you're in control, you feel confident.

As I said in Chapter 1, success in hockey and in life is about learning how to manage your mind. It is difficult to manage your thinking when your emotions are out of control (as they are when you are angry anxious, tired, or down). In this chapter I'll discuss the importance of creating right feelings — specifically, feelings of smoothness and power — and describe how breathing can help you to do that.

Breathing and "turning the wheel" can help you to energize, power up, attack, and make things happen. Breathing and releasing can help you to relax, regain your composure, increase your on-ice intelligence, and play smoothly.

"Attack" and "smooth" are the yin and yang of high-level hockey performance. Many players struggle to maintain the correct balance between the two. To play winning hockey you have to be able to energize, pump up, and attack, but also to calm down, regain composure, and play smoothly. The exact point where the two forces are in balance varies depending on a player's personality style, experience, position, and the role he plays.

The following graph illustrates the relationship between athletic performance and emotional arousal. It shows that, as emotional arousal or intensity increases (A) performance improves, until it peaks (B). Thereafter, increases in arousal (to the point of overarousal) cause people to get too pumped or tight, which leads to a reduction in performance (C).

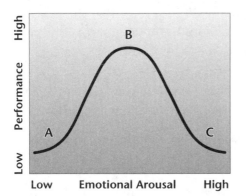

If you're not managing your emotions, it's hard to perform at your best. Under pressure, many players become anxious, they try too hard, force the play, squeeze their sticks, chase the puck, retaliate, make mistakes, and compound errors. Other players are flat and under-aroused. To excel, they need to increase their energy, intensity, and often their motivation. To my mind, the best and easiest way to control your emotional arousal and create right feelings is to learn how to use your breathing effectively.

Breathing

Most performance problems occur because the mind and body are not performing as one. Thoughts and feelings are not in sync. It often feels as if these two parts are not operating at the same speed. Usually, it seems that the mind is racing while the body lags behind. By focusing on breathing you can "get it together" and play smoothly.

When people feel anxious and worry, it's usually about the past or the future. They worry about mistakes they have made or mistakes they want to avoid. Worry lives in the past and future, but the power is in the present. By focusing on your breathing you bring your consciousness (mind) into the here-and-now world where the game of hockey is played. Remember: if you find yourself stuck in worrying about the past or the future, take a breath and bring your attention back to the present.

Our brains consist of two halves (the left and right cerebral cortex). Research indicates a smooth breathing rhythm can help you integrate left and right brain function. The left half of the brain processes logical, analytic, technical information. It helps you read the play and that reminds you to play your position. It says, "Pick up your check, come back hard, play the body, be patient." The right half of the brain deals more with feeling and coordination. It's the side that allows you to gap up, take the pass, and deflect a 90-mile-per-hour shot into the net. The right brain is more spontaneous and feeling-focused. It generates "soft hands" and the feeling of making the right moves.

Left Hemisphere	Right Hemisphere
thinking	*feeling*
analytic	*intuitive*
planning	*spontaneous*
past/future	*present*
words	*images*

Winning hockey requires a smooth, integrated functioning between the left and right cerebral hemispheres, between feeling and focus. It's about knowing what to do and doing it. It's about the left brain thinking clearly, but not too much. It's about the right brain managing feelings and not letting strong emotions take away your focus. Optimal performance occurs when these two halves of our brain perform in a coordinated and integrated fashion. Breathing smoothly can facilitate that and contribute to a high-performance state.

The complete player has both power and emotional control. Breathing is a key to both.

Exercise 1 ⇒

What follows is a simple breathing exercise that is basic to emotional control and "right feelings." It's one of the most important performance-enhancing aids I use.

To begin the process, sit back. I am going to ask you to experience three things in your breathing: *rhythm, inspiration,* and *direction.*

The most important part of breathing is noticing the rhythm of your breath. As you breathe, simply feel the breath come in . . . then feel the breath go out. Again, feel the breath come in . . . and feel the breath go out.

Spend a minute or two just experiencing your breathing.

The key to rhythm is time. Give yourself time for the in breath to come all the way in . . . then give yourself time for the out breath to flow all the way out . . . think of each breath as a wave in the ocean. And the waves never rush . . . Sit back. Relax. Give yourself time to feel the in breath flow in . . . and give yourself time to feel the out breath flow out.

It's very simple, but there is power in simplicity.

The second thing to focus on is the in breath. If breathing is respiration, then the in breath is the inspiration. To play winning hockey you want to be inspired. To inspire yourself, tune in to your breathing. Experience a smooth rhythm.

Now, as you breathe, place a little more emphasis on the in breath, on drawing in energy with each breath you take. Be aware that, wherever you are, there is energy all around you. Whether it's before a game, between periods, or on the bench between shifts, with each breath you can draw in some of that energy. You have a personal connection to an unlimited supply of energy. Tap it. Remember, first experience a smooth breathing rhythm. Then, draw in power.

The third key to breathing is direction. Once you have experienced a nice smooth rhythm and can feel yourself breathing in energy, the next step is to direct that energy. The direction can be internal or external. First, let's talk about directing your energy internally — that is, to your hands, feet, and eyes.

Feel yourself breathing in energy. Then imagine sending energy out through your shoulders and arms and into the palms of your hands. Imagine that, if you had a hockey stick in your hands, that energy would flow right into the shaft of the stick all the way down into the blade. Breathe smoothly and easily.

On the in breath, feel yourself breathing in energy. When you breathe out, feel or imagine energy flowing down into your hands and into your stick.

Next, picture yourself drawing in energy. This time, direct the flow of energy down through your hips and quads, into your calves, and down into the soles of your feet. Imagine that, if you had skates on, the energy would flow into the blades of the skates.

Once again, experience a smooth slow-breathing rhythm. As you breathe, feel yourself drawing in energy. This time, as you breathe out, imagine that you are sending energy up the spinal column, up into the head and into your eyes. Imagine yourself seeing clearly. You can see the open man. You have great peripheral vision. You can read the play . . . you can anticipate and react.

Exercise 2 ⇒

The feeling image we are developing is like a five-pointed star. It involves sending energy out into the hands, feet, and eyes.

Draw in energy and send it: out through the arms into the hands, and the stick, down through the legs into the feet, and skates, up into the head and the eyes, like a five-pointed star.

Success in hockey requires good hands, good wheels, and good eyes. Whether you play forward, defense, or goal, feeling like a five-pointed star can help you to excel. It's important to pair your feelings with your thoughts. As you breathe and direct the energy outward, think or say to yourself, "I am a star."

Cliff Ronning is an inspiring player. He's a little guy who, for 14 seasons, has weathered the battles of the NHL while averaging close to a point a game. When I first met Cliff six years ago, he impressed me as being a very motivated, intelligent player who cared a great deal about doing well. Cliff was playing well, but in spite of his success he worried about his performance, often running negative thoughts and focusing on past imperfections.

Cliff has led his team, the Nashville Predators, in scoring in each of the last three years. Recently, I asked him how the work we did together has helped his game. He told me he constantly goes over the areas we worked on.

"I'm always tuning in to my power thoughts and positive images of me playing well," he said. "I do it when things are going well and when they're going badly. One of the things I've learned over the years is that there are always going to be ups and downs and it's not a good idea to be too focused on the result. Instead, focus on doing the right things. Focus on getting a good feeling in your hands, feet, and eyes, and doing your ABCs, and the good results will come."

Cliff says that good feelings are important to playing well. "Sometimes when I'm playing, I'm able to create peace of mind. I think back to when I was a kid and I was just playing the game, loving the game, and having fun. When I can create that feeling, there's no pressure to score and no worry about money. I'm just working hard and having fun. That's when I play great.

"It's amazing to realize how much control you can actually have over your mind and how you can tune out the stupid or negative thoughts and images and focus on the basics that help you to succeed."

Cliff also says that self-esteem is important. Remembering and visualizing times when you did things well can build confidence. "It's a constant battle at this level to play well. There are so many good players. You can't take anything for granted. I think that the sport psychology training we've done has helped me to prepare better and focus on what's important . . . and tune out the rest."

Part of managing feelings has to do with being able to release feelings like tension and negativity. Tension is heavy. In a game like hockey, where speed and reaction are such a big piece of the puzzle, tension can be a tiring and limiting drag.

Exercise 3 ⟶

Learning how to release tension and negativity is important to playing well. Sit back, relax, and breathe. Now experience the contrasting feelings of tension and release in five key body areas. (You may wish to tape yourself reading this part aloud and then practice with the tape as a guide.)

Let's start with the **hands**. Create some tension in your hands by making fists. As you do, feel the tension in the central part of the hand and the fingers. Now turn your wrists inward so you feel an additional tension in the back of your hands. Hold that position for four seconds. Feel the tension. Now let go, release, and after you release, take a breath. It's that action of releasing and breathing that allows you to clear the screen and change channels on your mental TV. This is the feeling that you want to remember.

Our hands express our feelings. As I've said before, hockey players often squeeze the stick when they're trying too hard or when they're angry. What is ideal is to play with strong arms and soft hands. By soft hands I mean a feeling in the palms of your hands that facilitates your passing, shooting, and stickhandling ability.

One player I worked with, Dick, was a scrapper. He sometimes tried too hard and, in so doing, limited his touch around the net. Part of helping him handle the puck better was to teach him to release tightness and create soft feelings in his hands. At first the image of soft hands didn't appeal to Dick. He thought of his hands as weapons. I explained that when I said "soft hands" I was talking about the *palms* of his hands. "The backs of your hands can be like steel," I told him, "but think of yourself as having soft, scorer's hands." He understood the distinction and worked to develop his puck control skills.

The **neck** and **shoulders** are an area where most athletes tense when they're experiencing fear — whether it's fear of failure, embarrassment, or injury. It's a protective reflex, like the turtle pulling in its head when threatened. This response is limiting. It triggers a defensive, "watch out" reaction rather than a more confident, "go for it" attitude. Tightening in the neck and shoulders also interferes with breathing and reduces power and accuracy.

Raise your shoulders two or three inches. Hold that position for four seconds. Feel the tension? Now let go, release, and breathe. (Always release, then breathe.) Next, raise your shoulders just half an inch. It's hardly noticeable, but you can feel the tension. Notice that as you tense you cut down your breathing. Breath is power! Now release your shoulders, and after you do, take a breath.

Billy was a player who had a good shot. In practice, when he was loose, he could shoot hard and accurately. But he wasn't nearly as smooth or effective in games. Sure, he may have had less time to make a play in games than in practice, but when we watched videotapes of games we could both see that he just wasn't as smooth.

"Yeah," he said. "I get tighter in games. I try too hard. I don't want to miss a chance. And the more I try to avoid making a mistake, the tighter I get and the more I miss." One way to help Billy was to remind him that, any time he noticed tension in his neck and shoulders, he should release, breathe, and think *smooth.*

Check your body for tension from time to time. If you notice it in the neck, shoulders, or hands, remember to release and breathe. Always release and breathe.

As you practice relaxing and breathing, place one hand on your **chest** and the other on your **abdomen**. Feel these parts of your body expand and contract with each breath you take. I've compared the act of breathing to the motion of waves in the ocean. Breathe easily, and feel the waves rise and fall with each breath you take. Part of your pregame preparation or postgame relaxation could include relaxed breathing with hands on the chest and abdomen.

The **crotch** or genital region is another tension-holding area. To create tension in the crotch, squeeze that sphincter muscle you tighten when you avoid going to the toilet. As you squeeze that muscle, notice that it impedes your breathing. Hold it for four seconds, then release and take a breath. The point to remember is that you can tense or release any part of your body. You're the boss. You're in control. And an important part of generating right feelings is to learn to scan the body for tension and let it go. Holding tension anywhere is an obstacle to breathing, power, and performance.

Lastly, curl your toes. Make fists with your **feet**, like a bird holding onto a perch. As you do, take note of the tension in your feet. Hold for four seconds, then release and take a breath. Think about cat's feet — cats have great balance and acceleration.

Take a few relaxed breaths. As you do, feel yourself drawing in energy and sending it out to your hands, your feet, and your eyes. Feel energy flowing through you like a five-pointed star. Now scan your body. If any part of your body still feels tense, think of that part of your body as you release and breathe. Again, breathe in energy and allow it to flow through you. Allow yourself to feel powerful. Allow yourself to be a star. What I have just described is a simple, effective technique for creating feelings of smoothness and ease that will help you use your energy effectively.

The release reflex is a key to your mental management. It's how you'll clear the screen on your mental TV. The components of the release reflex are being aware, releasing, and breathing. You can use the release reflex to get rid of unnecessary tension and negative thoughts, to stay lighter, and to have greater control over your emotions. Remember, feelings affect thinking. If you are feeling tense, angry, or tight, you must release, breathe, and clear the screen. Change your feeling and your focus. Create a new, positive, power thought. Be a star.

Exercise 4 ⇒

All right, now let's relate these feelings to hockey . . . Breathe smoothly and breathe in energy . . . Feel the energy flowing through you like a five-pointed star.

Imagine that you are about to step onto the ice . . . Feel yourself sending energy out to your hands . . . Imagine having good hands and being able to handle the puck well, to make good tape-to-tape passes, and take quick, hard, accurate shots.

Feel yourself breathing in energy and sending it down to your legs . . . Imagine having good wheels . . . You feel strong on your skates and you are skating with smoothness and power . . . You have good acceleration and jump.

Breathe in energy and send it up into your eyes . . . Imagine that you see the ice clearly . . . You read the play well. You see the open man and the open space . . . You anticipate their play, angle your man to the outside, and take the puck away.

Empowerment is a concept that has become popular in recent years. I define power as energy for work; a key to being empowered is to tune in to your breathing and draw in energy. Then direct that energy and allow it to flow through your body. Empowerment is feeling and knowing you are charged, in control, and ready to work.

Marg was a talented young center, a smart player who skated well and had good hands and a good shot. However, like many hockey players, she would think too much and about too many things when she was under pressure. Often, her thinking was negative, about the things she did "wrong." This focus caused her to be tense, slowed her reactions, and reduced her touch. The more Marg struggled, the more she worried and the more tense she became. She worried that she wasn't scoring, that if she didn't produce she would get less ice time. The more Marg worried, the less productive she became — and the less ice time she saw. It was a vicious cycle.

The first step in helping Marg turn her game around was to teach her to release and breathe, to create good feelings and a positive focus. Because Marg had an active mind and tended to worry, I showed her how to use that worry as a reminder to take a breath and focus on positive feelings and positive plays. Gradually, Marg became better able to change her feelings and to manage her mind. As she did, her performance improved dramatically.

Breathing is a key to managing your mind. It's a key to filling yourself with energy and power. Power is a force that will work for you. Tap the mains. Draw in energy. Let energy flow through you. Be a star.

Scott Gomez is a player I consulted with for a couple of years when he was playing junior hockey in the British Columbia and Western hockey leagues. He went on to enjoy a sensational rookie season with the New Jersey Devils, which culminated in his being named the NHL's rookie of the year for 1999–2000. Scott uses breathing to relax before games. "Sometimes I get so excited about the game, I can't even take a nap," he says. "That's when I think of the waves, and of breathing slowly and smoothly. It can really help me calm down and get to sleep. Sometimes I combine that breathing with imagining myself playing well."

Scott also uses breathing between shifts, when he's on the bench. "I use my breathing both to calm down and to energize," he says. "If I notice I'm angry or frustrated, I take a breath. When I was playing junior I was yelled at for snapping. I remembered to take a breath, to stay cool and remember my ABCs. It all starts with that first breath; it helps you to refocus and stay in control. The breathing stuff has been tremendous help to me. It's important to be in control."

Mark Hardy saw action as a defenseman in more than 900 games, most of them with the Los Angeles Kings, for whom he's now an assistant coach. Mark says: "When I was playing, the biggest thing for me was to be in control. I wanted to play with intensity, but I also wanted to have control. Control would allow me to go into the corner and be physical. It would help me stay calm and focused, make the right reads, and not chase the puck like a chicken with its head cut off. Breathing helped me to have control." Like Scott Gomez, Mark used breathing to relax before games, combining it with visualization to get ready to play. He also used it on the bench to collect his thoughts and try to stay in control during games. "When I needed to, I used it to elevate my intensity," Mark says. "And I used it after the game to calm down and help me to focus on the good things I had done."

Energize by Turning the Wheel

We've seen that breathing is a way to calm down, regain your composure, and play smooth hockey. It's also a way to energize, get pumped up and ready to attack.

The game of hockey demands energy, and there are many ways to energize. Some players listen to music, some take a cold shower, some exercise, some visualize themselves playing good hockey, and some talk positively or aggressively to themselves. In my opinion, there is no more basic and powerful way than to learn to use your breathing and "turn the wheel."

Exercise 5 ➡

Once again, focus on your breathing. This time, picture the breath as a wheel turning. On the in breath, the wheel turns up (A). On the out breath, the wheel turns down (B).

Right now, you are relatively relaxed, so the wheel turns slowly. As you skate, your heart and respiratory rates increase and the wheel turns faster and faster. Still, on the in breath the wheel turns up, and on the out-breath it turns down.

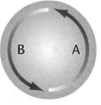

Spend a minute or two experiencing your breath as a wheel turning.

As the wheel turns, it generates power. You are a power generator. It's a physical reality that, as you breathe and turn the wheel, you generate power. As your heart beats and your lungs expand and contract you are pumping blood, oxygen, and energy out through the body. You are generating power. For a moment, imagine yourself turning the wheel.

Breathe in energy, feel the wheel turn up. Breathe out, feel the wheel turn down. Feel the wheel turn up, and draw in energy and power. Then feel the wheel turn down, and send out the power.

Turning the wheel is a force that you can use to pump yourself up and send your energy out — remember the five-pointed star. It's important to direct your energy. Send it out to the hands, to the feet, and to the eyes.

Good hands. Pump up, turn the wheel. Breathe in energy and send it out to your hands. Imagine energy flowing right into the shaft and the blade of your stick. Imagine that feeling of good hands and having great stick control. Visualize yourself with great stick control.

Good wheels. Turn the wheel again. Breathe in energy, and this time send it down through your hips and legs into the soles of your feet — cat's feet. Imagine skating well, feeling strong on your skates, having good balance and jump — having good wheels. Imagine skating with speed and power.

Good eyes. Finally, turn the wheel, draw in energy, and send it up into your eyes. Imagine that you can see very clearly. You can see the open man and the open space. You can anticipate the play and react almost before things happen.

Now, imagine being on the bench. Your shift is up next. You want to be charged and ready. You remember to breathe, turn the wheel, draw in energy, and generate power. You send it into your hands and stick — good hands. Down into your legs and feet — good wheels — and up into your eyes — good eyes. Imagine stepping onto the ice charged and focused. You're the boss. You control your feelings. If you find you are squeezing the stick, forcing the play, or feeling too tight, then use your breathing and streaming to create smooth feelings and being a star.

If you want energy to attack, turn the wheel. Whether you've been sitting on the bench the entire period or you're double-shifting and you need a lift, breathe in energy, turn the wheel, and send power down through the drive train, through the arms into the hands, and up into the eyes. Then think positive and imagine yourself playing well.

Over the years I have recommended this technique of turning the wheel and sending energy to hands, feet, and eyes to hundreds of hockey players. Here's how three veterans used the technique.

Jamie was an experienced NHL defenseman who, after nine seasons in the league, had been relegated to a backup role. When I met him, he was only getting about five minutes of ice time a game and only one or two shifts a period. He told me that, even though he prepared himself well before the game, his energy level would drop after sitting for 10, 12, or 15 minutes and it was hard for him to stay psyched up and feeling ready to go when called on. He asked if I could suggest a technique to help him "feel more ready" for those few minutes in each game when he would be asked to excel.

I showed Jamie how to use his breathing to turn the wheel and generate power while he sat on the bench, and how to send energy out into his hands, feet, and eyes. I suggested that he do that exercise every five minutes, explaining to him that when he felt energized (like a star), he should watch the defenseman playing his position and imagine that *he* was out on the ice, making all the right plays — playing the man, stepping up, making the pass, jumping up into the rush, and taking the shot.

Dan was an NHL veteran and all-star who got a great deal of ice time. After we had done some training, he confided to me that he was concerned about something: when he came off the ice after a hard shift, he would have trouble keeping his mind on the game. I explained to him that it was quite normal for players coming off the ice to find it hard to concentrate on the game until they had first caught their breath and then reorganized.

Exhaustion or oxygen debt is disorienting. After a player has a full, hard shift on the ice, he needs to regroup for the next shift. The natural way to do that when you come off the ice is simply to catch your breath. To do that, tune in to your breathing rhythm. Once you can breathe smoothly and easily again, you are better able to concentrate effectively, think about drawing in energy and feel like a star. Then you're ready to focus on externals such as the play on the ice and getting your head right back into the game. That whole refocusing process can take just a minute.

In his biography, NHL tough guy Dave "Tiger" Williams relates a story from the Canucks' 1982 playoff run that took them all the way to the Stanley Cup finals. As Tiger describes it, he was sitting on the bench during the third period of game two. He was tired and his legs didn't feel good. "I needed to really bear down and produce some energy. I had to get the goddamned stuff from somewhere," he writes. He recalls that he thought about the things we had talked about, as well as his mother, who had always been a source of energy for him. He describes asking for energy and taking a few breaths. As he says in the book, "When the game went into overtime, I got the energy and I got the winning goal."[1]

Power Words

We have discussed breathing as waves and as a wheel. The rule of thumb is to breathe like waves when you want to smooth things out and turn the wheel when you want to attack.

People are different. Some players need to calm down, while others need to energize or pump up. It's important for you to assess and become aware of who you are and what you need to do to perform at your best. Determine whether there's an approach to right feelings that might be beneficial to you, and discover when and how you can best implement it.

One thing I want you to add to your high-performance feelings is a power word. A power word can help you to shape your energy, especially when you pair it with your feelings. The word you choose depends on who you are and what you want. If the feeling you want to experience is smoothness and improved touch and coordination, use the word *smooth*. If you find yourself pushing too hard or playing too tight, while generating smooth feelings think of the

---

1 Dave Williams and James Lawton, *Tiger: A Hockey Story*, (Vancouver: Douglas & McIntyre, 1984).

word *smooth*. If the feeling you want is speed, turn the wheel and think a word like *fast* or *jump*. Breathe, turn the wheel, and imagine skating at about three-quarters speed; then, picture yourself accelerating, speeding up, and blowing past people. Think fast. On the other hand, if your energy is down and you want to feel more pumped and aggressive — to generate more energy to forecheck aggressively or go to the net — think of the word *attack*. Thinking *attack* works whether you're on offense or on defense. And away from the rink, if you want to generate power for a workout in the gym, you can also turn the wheel and think *attack*.

One player I worked with, Larry, was very skeptical about breathing exercises. "I just don't see how taking a few breaths is going to help me to play better hockey," he told me. Later he would confide that he thought the whole idea of sport psychology was useless. Then one day he tried to use breathing for his strength workouts in the gym. He suddenly realized how much more power he could generate if he focused on his breathing. After that experience it made perfect sense to bring that skill with him onto the ice. He started to use breathing and the thought of attacking into his battles along the boards and whenever he drove to the net.

Another player, Hugo, was a talented, highly motivated junior with the talent to make the pros. He came to see me because, as he put it, "I'm in a slump." When I asked what he meant, he replied, "Something weird is happening to me. I don't feel good on the ice and I'm not scoring any goals."

When I asked him to put a finger on what specifically he was not feeling good about on the ice, he said that he was normally a very good skater, but he was feeling slow. He also felt that he didn't have a good touch around the net.

I decided to check for any health issues. When I asked Hugo how he felt away from the ice, he said he felt fine, was sleeping and eating normally. "It's just that I don't feel as fast and as sharp," he said, "and I've been missing the chances I've been getting."

"What does it feel like when you're playing great?" I asked him.

Without hesitating, he replied, "I feel quick, confident, and sharp. And I put the puck in the net."

"Do you think that maybe you're pressing, or trying too hard?"

"Yeah, I probably am," said Hugo. "I've got to get drafted this year."

I asked him to tell me about a time when he felt he was playing great hockey. He thought for a moment, then said that he had scored eight goals in the past year's playoffs. And he had been off to a good start this season.

"Tell me again," I said, "what does it feel like when you're playing well?"

"I told you," he replied. "I feel fast, sharp, and confident."

It was time to pose an important question. "Instead of having to play great and score goals in order to feel good, what if you were to create those good feelings first — do you think that you would play better and score more?"

"Yeah, I probably would," he said. "Yeah, sure."

"Then why," I asked, "do you create those other tense, slow feelings?"

"I'm not doing it on purpose," Hugo protested.

"But you are doing it, Hugo. You're the boss. If I were to show you, or remind you, how to feel good on the ice, would that help?"

Sure it would, he said, and he asked me to show him how to feel good.

Now that I had Hugo's full attention, I told him a bit about how the mind worked — how tension can create negative feelings and negative thoughts, which in turn create more negative feelings. And how tension makes people feel slow, tight, and tired.

That rang a bell for Hugo. "Yeah," he said. "I have been feeling really tired at the end of my shifts."

Over the course of the next two sessions I showed him how to use his breathing to create more ease and power, and how to let that power flow out like a star. I told him that, whenever he felt tense or tired, he should take a breath, turn the wheel and generate power, and send energy out to his hands, feet, and eyes. "The game is hands, feet, and eyes," I told him.

One way that Hugo could avoid having those heavy feelings was to practice his breathing every day on and off the ice, I said. And I promised him that, if he practiced creating *smooth* and *fast* feelings, it wouldn't be long before he would be feeling fast, sharp, and confident again. I reiterated to Hugo that he was the boss and that he created his feelings. If he didn't like the way he felt, it was up to him to change the channel and create other feelings.

Hugo followed that advice. He practiced breathing daily, both on and off the ice. He imagined himself being smooth, light, and fast, making all his good moves. Before long, Hugo was playing like Hugo again.

In this chapter I have emphasized the importance of creating right feelings — specifically, feelings of smoothness and power — and how to use breathing to help you to be calm, centered, and powerful. As I said earlier, creating the winning hockey performance state is about combining right feelings with right focus.

If:

State = Feeling + Focus

Then:

High-Performance State = Right Feeling + Right Focus

Everyone is a performer. You will perform better as a hockey player by being clear about your on-ice focus. Power programs are a way of improving your focus; they include the power thoughts, images, and feelings you bring to mind to help yourself react and excel. In the next three chapters we'll look at enhancing your power programs and explore the thoughts, images, and attitude that will help you to do that.

Tiger Williams says of sport psychology: "In my experience it's another tool that a player can use to be better. When I played, they only trained the body, not the mind. Sport psychology can teach you how to focus. Many coaches tell you to 'focus,' but many young athletes really don't know what that means."

HOMEWORK ⸺➤

There are seven homework assignments for Chapter 2.

Assignment 1 ⸺➤

Work with your breathing (refer back to Exercises 1 through 4). Create a 10-minute breathing session every day. Sit or lie back, get into your breathing, experience a smooth-breathing rhythm (one in which the waves flow in and the waves flow out). As you achieve that rhythm, emphasize the in breath, with which you draw in energy, then feel that energy flow out through the body like a five-pointed star.

Assignment 2 ⸺➤

After about five minutes of relaxed breathing, spend the next two or three minutes imagining yourself on the ice, skating with smoothness, power, and ease. If you are a forward or defenseman, imagine handling the puck well, making good passes, and having good touch and a hard, accurate shot. Imagine playing good defense, playing the man and finishing your checks. If you are a goalie, imagine having good position and angles, seeing the shooter, stopping each shot, and moving well in the net.

Assignment 3 ⸺➤

On the ice, experience yourself breathing in energy and feeling energy flow through you. When you come off the ice at the end of your shift, pick up your breathing for eight breaths. Just watch 10 breaths flow in and flow out. On breath number 4, imagine the energy flowing out through your arms and hands. On breath number 5, your legs and feet. On number 6, up through the spinal column into your head and eyes. Then spend the last few breaths imagining the five-pointed star.

Assignment 4 ➡

While you stretch before a game or practice, remember to release
and breathe. Combining breathing with stretching can give you more
release, and give your muscles more oxygen, more energy, and a
better stretch.

Assignment 5 ➡

In practice — or if you are riding a stationary bike or running —
experience "breathing as a wheel." Pay particular attention to turning
the wheel and generating power whenever you experience fatigue, just
before you step onto the ice.

Assignment 6 ➡

Begin working to get a sense of whether you are someone who could
benefit more by smoothing or by attacking. Begin to practice shifting
gears and powering up or down by using your breathing.

Assignment 7 ➡

Define three or four power words that you can use when you play.
Practice combining these words with your breathing.

Chapter 3

Power Thoughts: Think It, Do It

The power thoughts you choose to put on your mental TV directly affect how you perform on the ice. There are three kinds of power thoughts you can use to enhance your on-ice performance: feeling thoughts, strategy thoughts, and affirmations.

Feeling Thoughts

The first kind of power thoughts are the feeling thoughts we have been discussing over the last two chapters. Feeling thoughts include "good hands," "good wheels," and "good eyes."

As you think a feeling thought, allow yourself to feel or experience it. *Good hands* thinking can include "Soft hands . . . good touch . . . dangling . . . the puck's on a string . . . snapping off quick accurate shots and passes." Think these thoughts, and make sure you feel them, too.

Examples of *good wheels* thinking can include "Feet moving . . . I'm strong on my skates . . . I have good speed and good jump." Or it can include power skating thoughts like "Stay square . . . low in the knees . . . extend the stride . . . full power, full length . . . turn and burn."

Good eyes thinking includes "Head up . . . head on a swivel . . . good reads . . . see and anticipate . . . know who's where . . . find the open man . . . the open space."

A second kind of feeling thought relates to your intensity level. As we said earlier, there's an optimal intensity level at which each player excels. Feeling either too aroused or too calm can interfere with your playing at your best. You are response-able to keep yourself in your optimal arousal zone. Optimal arousal levels vary for each player. Discover your own.

Moe was a scorer who found himself getting into foolish fights that took him off the ice. He was a high-arousal player with a low flash point. If he made a mistake, or if somebody hit him, he would get frustrated and angry and he would overreact. As a result, he would take thoughtless, selfish penalties that forced his team to work harder. Helping him to be calm wasn't simply a matter of explaining that a thoughtless reaction was selfish. For Moe to be able to manage his temper (or his arousal level), he would have to learn to take a breath and think *smooth*. Affirmations such as "I'm a scorer, not a scrapper" were also very helpful. I'll say more about affirmations later in this chapter.

I was playing a round of golf with an NHL defenseman. He knew I'd worked with PGA Tour players and asked me to help him with his golf game. "How can I be more consistent?" he asked.

After observing him play I replied, "Don't try so hard."

"What do you mean?" he asked.

"I mean, feel the shot. Don't be so caught up with results. You're either trying to crush the ball to make it go an extra twenty yards down the fairway, or you're trying to avoid the rough or the bunker. In both cases this 'trying' causes tension that reduces coordination and timing."

"What am I supposed to do?" he asked.

"Think smooth. Take a breath and think about hitting through the ball *smooth* and sweet. Then, the ball will probably go where you want it to. It's the same in hockey." I added, "Whether you're shooting from the point or the top of the circle, consistency comes from being smooth and not trying to shoot too hard."

Rick Lanz was a defenseman with the Vancouver Canucks and Toronto Maple Leafs for several years during the mid 1980s, when Wayne Gretzky was at his peak. What made Gretzky so effective? "It was his ability to be calm ['smooth'] under pressure," Rick says. "He could hold the puck and take a look — and when he'd do that he would force you to make the first move." Feeling and thinking *smooth* can add to your on-ice intelligence and finish. Feeling and thinking *attack* can generate opportunity. Excellence is about balance. Learn when to *attack* and when to *smooth*.

Strategy Thoughts and Your ABCs

The second kind of power thoughts are strategy thoughts. The simplest strategy is to keep your eye on the puck. Of course, when it comes to reading the game and reacting well, there's more to it than watching the puck: there's making the right reads, anticipating the play, and playing the system. Strategy thoughts can help you sharpen your on-ice judgment and reactions and stay focused. For example, strategy thoughts for playing good defense in a penalty-killing situation might include:

A. Be aggressive but patient. Don't commit.
B. Maintain good position and good angles.
C. Clear the front of the net.
(and even D. Head on a swivel and stick on the ice.)

What is really important is that you be clear about what you want to do on the ice. That clarity should be reflected in a simple power thought. Indeed, these strategy thoughts should be so clear that just saying the thought to yourself brings an image of that action to mind.

Your "ABCs" should be so clear that you can actually visualize them. Let me give you two examples. Dave was a winger, a grinder, with the Chicago Blackhawks. When I met him he worked very hard, both to get a few shifts a game and to win battles along the boards during those shifts. Because of his limited ice time, Dave worried about making the right impression on each and every shift. The trouble was he would try too hard, which limited his impact.

I began working with Dave on his breathing and to increase his body awareness and ease. Then, we reviewed his ABCs. Dave was a big guy with a tendency from time to time to stand around and watch the play. He had to remind himself to keep his feet moving. Not surprisingly, point A for Dave was "Keep my feet moving." Task B was "Win the puck on the boards." Dave also had to be sure to manage his defensive responsibilities — cover his check and get the puck out of his end. So Dave selected "Get the puck out of our end" as chore C. Thereafter, whenever Dave worried what the coach was thinking, he reminded himself to take a breath, remember his ABCs, and refocus on executing them. Being clear about what he had to do, and focusing on it, seemed to reduce Dave's anxiety and increase his impact. To review, Dave's ABCs were:

A. **Keep my feet moving.**
B. **Win the puck on the boards.**
C. **Get the puck out of our end.**

Morris Lukowich had been a high-scoring left-winger with the Winnipeg Jets for several years. After a series of injuries and trades, he was aquired by the Los Angeles Kings. They gave him a chance to play on the power play. It was a pressure-filled assignment that presented a real challenge. Morris knew that if he didn't produce, his career might be over. He was nervous.

After helping him to relax, I asked him to list his ABCs — the three things he'd have to do to be successful on the power play. I told him that his ABCs should be specific and clear enough that he could picture them. He thought for a moment, then he said:

A. I have to get the puck in my corner.

B. I have to make good passes, both to the center
in the slot and to the point.

C. I have to take good shots.

"Can you picture doing each of these ABCs?" I asked.

Yes, he said, he could see it. "A, get the puck in my corner — I'm like a cat pouncing on the mouse. B, make good passes — I can see myself passing to the center in the slot and to the man at the point. I can even visualize who is playing these positions." And he named the players. "And C, take a scoring shot — that's something I can feel in my hands more than I can visualize it."

Here's a diagram of Morris's power-play ABCs:

A. Get the puck in the corner.

B. Make good passes to the center (B1) or the point (B2).

C. Take an accurate shot.

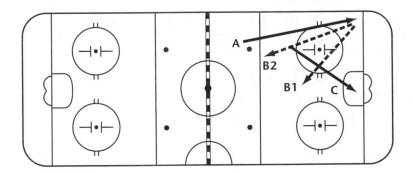

Curt Fraser, the head coach of the Atlanta Thrashers and a former NHL winger, was asked what it takes to play in the NHL. "You have to know exactly what you want to do in every zone and in every aspect of the game. You have to focus on the details."[1] (The ABCs.)

Do you know your ABCs? They are an important key to developing a clear focus and playing winning hockey. They represent the specifics of what you should do in each situation. Create a clear

1 Curt Fraser interviewed on The Team, 1040 Radio, May 18, 2001.

thought and diagram for what you would do in each of the following situations.

What do you do when your team is attacking and has the puck in its own end?

A. _____

B. _____

C. _____

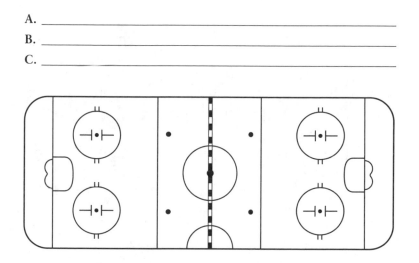

What do you do when you're defending and they have the puck in your end?

A. _____

B. _____

C. _____

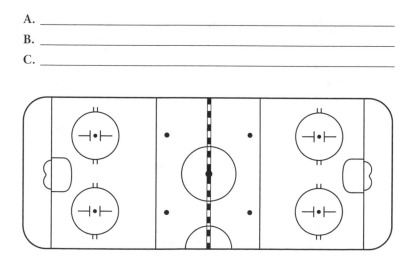

If you are on special teams, what do you do on the power play? Or when your team is killing a penalty?

A. _____

B. _____

C. _____

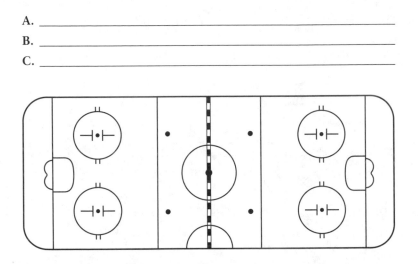

A veteran winger for the St. Louis Blues approached me after I had given a talk to the team. He was both a checker and a scorer. I had talked about focusing, but because he played different roles on different lines he was unsure what his ABCs should be. It was a hockey strategy question — one best answered by a coach, not a sport psychologist. But I understood his uncertainty, so I told him: "You're an intelligent guy. It's important for you to be clear about your ABCs and your on-ice focus. And that's something that you really have to discuss with the coaching staff."

He agreed to talk with them later, and left the room. As he did, one of the coaches approached me with a smile and said, "You know, Saul, I think that's the first time anyone ever told him he was intelligent."

I replied, "If you want him to play intelligent hockey, then you should tell him he is intelligent. And also help him to be clear about his ABCs."

Too often, coaches are critical of a player in a way that leads the player to think he's not smart, that he's incapable of playing intelligent hockey. Players will be more successful if they hold the image of the player they want to be, talk positively to themselves, and focus on the specifics of what they want to do. Coaches will be more successful if they have a sense of who they want their players to be, talk positively to them, and are specific about what they want them to do.

In coaching yourself, and others, my ABC advice is that you:

A. **Define clear directions (your ABCs). Know what you have to do on the ice.**
B. **Find positive things to acknowledge about your performance.**
C. **Always analyze the behavior — not the person.**

By that last point I mean that, if a player misses an assignment, don't run him down (by saying, "You're stupid" or "What the hell is wrong with you?"). Instead, provide the player with feedback about what he did — or didn't do — that was unacceptable, and demand more. Tell him he is capable of better play (e.g., "That's a poor decision. You're smarter than that. You're responsible to cover the front of the net. Communicate. You know you don't go into the corner when there's no coverage in front of the net."). Clear ABCs and positive power thinking are essential to increasing on-ice productivity.

One interesting observation about ABCs. Over the two decades I've been working with NHLers, I have had the chance to discuss the ABCs of scoring with many players. (I'll relate some of their responses in Chapter 11.) The scoring power thought that I heard most often was "A. Shoot the puck."

Affirmations

Affirmations are positive statements you can say to yourself to give yourself strength. Remember, you get more of what you think about. Affirmations can strengthen your attitude, identity, and confidence. Some examples of affirmations include thoughts like "I'm the boss"; "I control my reactions"; "One shift at a time"; "I read the play well"; "I control the front of the net"; "I have a great goal-scoring reflex." And, for goalies, "I can stop everything I see."

I frequently make tapes for athletes in which I combine instructions for relaxation and breathing with power thoughts. To choose thoughts that will work well for you, you must first explore how you want to feel, then define what you want to achieve. Once you've completed these two steps, you will be able to create an affirmation or power thought that you feel comfortable and positive about saying to yourself. These statements should be credible to you — and positive.

The following is a list of affirmations that I prepared for Los Angeles Kings players. They were encouraged to select between six and ten power thoughts from the list and incorporate them into their self-talk.

On the tape, I would remind the players to take a breath after each thought. I would also point out that thought precedes action, so they should think positive, and that repetition build strength, so they would get the best results by thinking these thoughts repeatedly.

- I'm the boss (of my mental TV).
- I make a difference on every shift.
- I have a personal connection to an unlimited supply of energy.
- Any time, with just a breath, I can feel more calm, focused, and powerful. (Remember to breathe . . . especially if you are feeling tense or nervous.)
- A little adrenaline and some breathing are like jet fuel.
- I'm a star. Energy flows through me like a star (a five-pointed star).
- I am attack and smooth.
- I am very talented.
- I am quick and strong like a cat (a tiger, a panther).
- I am strong on my skates.
- I have great jump.
- I have an accurate shot.

- I have a great goal-scoring reflex.
- I love to score goals.
- I am a tough, aggressive checker.
- I am unbeatable when I play the body.
- The more I hit, the sharper I get.
- I enjoy a challenge. I enjoy checking the great ones.
- I use everything for power and focus.
- I am a winner. We are winners.
- I am committed. I am willing to do whatever is necessary to achieve our goal.
- I am mentally tough.
- My mind is a force I use to make things happen.
- I get stronger, tougher, and sharper with each shift.
- Self-acceptance means allowing myself to win.

Exercise 1 ⇒

Review the preceding list of affirmations and determine which ones might work for you. By that I mean select those that are credible to you, that address your strengths or aspects of your game that you want to develop, or those that just feel good to you. Select the six to 10 affirmations or power thoughts that would most help you to become a more powerful, positive player. Or make up your own affirmations using the Kings' list as a reference. Write your affirmations down and say them to yourself often.

Affirmations can be in the first person ("*I* am smooth, *I* am a power machine"), a format which is personal and powerful. Or you can affirm in the second person ("*You* are a star, *you* use everything"). In our day-to-day lives, people usually address us in the second person. It's effective — and pleasant — to hear positive things said about us in the second person. I often make tapes for athletes repeating affirmations in both ways.

Words are like food for the spirit. Words can nurture us. Just as you wouldn't eat foods you didn't like or that didn't taste right, part of being the complete player is saying things to yourself that feel good to you and that give you power.

And repetition builds strength. In the weight room, repetitions of a simple physical exercise build muscle. It's the same with affirmations and power thoughts. Repeat your power words and thoughts to yourself frequently.

Develop your positive mental focus and attitude. Whether you're relaxed or facing a challenge, take a breath and affirm the positive. Remember to choose power thoughts that create a feeling and a picture that increases your confidence, direction, and sense of what is possible.

Linda had been a hard-working winger on a collegiate team — a national champion. She was preparing for a training camp in the women's professional hockey league. She described herself as a solid checker. When I asked her about her offensive prowess, she said, "I can score in practice, but not in games."

I pointed out to Linda that part of being a complete player is to be aware of your self-talk and maintain a positive focus. I asked her to consider what she had just said about herself. It might be that she is more of a checker than a scorer, I said, but if she was ever going to develop her scoring ability it was crucial that she change the way she talked and thought about herself.

I told her: "I'm not suggesting that you see yourself stickhandling through the other team like Forsberg or Gretzky, turn on the jets and blow past the defense like Bure or Kariya, or shoot like MacInnis or Hull. However, you are strong along the boards. See yourself winning the puck on the boards and working the give-and-go. See yourself making the pass to the center high in the slot or to the point, then skating to the net, getting the pass, and shooting and scoring."

I told Linda to talk to herself, saying things like "The puck is mine. I will win the puck on the boards. I execute the give-and-go very effectively. I have a good shot from in close. Scoring is just part of my working hard."

"Affirm and imagine these abilities," I said. "Practice the give-

and-go off the boards and work on your shot in practice. Be a positive self-talker. Be a more complete player. Be a checker and a scorer."

Another example: John was a young player who admitted to playing poorly when his father came to the rink to watch him play. He said his dad was a stern critic who always focused on what he did wrong, and his presence caused John to feel uptight. I told him it was quite a common problem; I have seen many NHL players, especially those on the fringe, become unfocused from trying to impress the coach.

I told John that the best antidote to the "dis-ease" of having a critic watch you play and wait for you to make a mistake is to be clear about what you want to do and be positive when you talk to yourself.

Kenny was a defenseman who was struggling to make the Edmonton Oilers. He came to see me prior to his second training camp. He recalled having had a terrible training camp the season before because, as he put it, "I was totally focused on what the coach was thinking instead of on my own positive thoughts. I was worried all the time. I wondered if the coach had seen me make that pass, if he saw me miss my check. I would wonder why he changed my defense partner. I worried about everything.

"Bottom line, I became a nervous wreck. Instead of being positive and focusing on my job on the ice, I was focusing on what was going on in the coach's head. I didn't play well. And I don't want to repeat that situation this year."

We started out working on his breathing. Then I reminded Kenny to start thinking "I'm the boss" and "I'm a star." He came to see himself as someone with good wheels, good hands, and good eyes. Then he defined his on-ice ABCs. Finally, he affirmed that he could execute his ABCs effectively and confidently. He repeated thoughts like:

A. **I make good reads and I maintain good position.**
B. **I'm strong and smart, and I clear the front of the net.**
   The front of the net is mine.
C. **I make good passes and I get the puck out of our end.**

I introduced Kenny to the release reflex and I explained that anytime he had a worrisome or negative thought, he should take a breath, release the negativity, and think of one of his positive thoughts. "Kenny," I said, "you're an intelligent guy with an active mind. That's a plus. If you have a worrisome thought, use it to remind yourself to take a breath and focus on your positive ABCs. Think positive. You get more of what you think about." He did and he had a great camp.

When should you use positive thoughts? All the time, I think. When you are aware that your thoughts are negative, change them to positive, power thoughts. Remember, you get more of what you think about. Positive thinking works. Some players report that being too thoughtful immediately before and during a game slows them down. They prefer to be in the moment, to react and create. Others have found that repeating their ABCs and affirmations before a game increases their focus and confidence. Define your ABCs. Create some power thoughts. Then find out, based on your experience, when doing your mental reps works best for you.

The use of power words can be extremely helpful in dealing with the pressure and challenges that are a part of every sport — including hockey. The following non-hockey anecdote is one of my favorites, and is an excellent example of how power words can be used to help a group of athletes (in this case, cyclists) achieve a remarkable result.

I have worked with Canada's national cycling team since the early 1980s. One of my challenges was helping the national TTT (team time trial) cyclists qualify and prepare for the Olympics. Team time trial is an event in which four men ride down the highway in a straight line, one behind the other, racing against the clock for 100 kilometers. The first rider in the line encounters most of the air resistance and expends 25 percent more energy than the rest. After about 40 seconds to a minute in the lead — about the same duration as a hockey shift — he tires and slips back to fourth place, while the second rider moves up to take the lead. After another 40-second "shift" the new leader tires, slips back to fourth, and the cyclist who started in third place moves into the lead. And so it goes, a grueling trek across the countryside, each cyclist taking a turn in the lead and pressing to maintain the pace.

I worked with the TTT riders for a week at the beginning of their season in early March, showing them techniques for greater ease, focus, and control. Then they went off to train and race in Texas, Europe, and in the Rocky Mountains. When I met them again in British Columbia in early July, they were in excellent shape. They had been well coached and well conditioned, and had been given very good equipment.

This is the ideal basis for a sport psychologist to work from. It is possible to influence the psyche of an athlete who's not in very good shape, but in a physically demanding 100-kilometer race all the motivation and focus in the world won't make much difference if the athlete lacks the necessary physical conditioning or the proper equipment. However, when athletes are physically and technically prepared, getting them mentally up to speed can make a tremendous difference.

Once the Canadian Cycling Association had selected the Olympic team, the Olympic Committee (an independent body) had to approve the selections. Their job was to ensure that all athletes sent to the Olympic Games would be competitive, and they refused to send performers — even if they were the best in the country — who were not up to world standards. The Olympic Committee had set a standard of 2 hours, 5 minutes, 30 seconds for the TTT team to meet. The Canadian record was 2:06:40. In effect, the committee was telling these prospective Olympians that they shave a minute and 10 seconds off the best time ever or they would not go to the Olympics.

As usual, I began my work with the cyclists by showing them how to breathe and release tension. In cycling, as in hockey, tension is a drag — it slows you down. We worked individually and in groups. As the riders became more relaxed and focused, I asked them what thoughts and feelings they experienced that limited them when they raced. Essentially, they described three limiting thoughts or "programs." They had to do with fear, pain, and difficulty. These same limiting thoughts also apply to hockey players.

The fear the racers spoke about was a fear of failure and embarrassment, fear of losing control, of breaking down, and the fear of crashing and injury. For most of us, fear is a high-frequency performance thought. It's one that can mobilize us into action or, as we saw in Chapter 1, it can cause contraction, limit breathing, and cut down power.

The pain experienced in cycling is a physical pain so intense at times that a rider can't continue to race. Some even pass out on their bicycles. There is also the psychic pain that racers — and non-riders — experience when they entertain the possibility of failing. Psychic pain threatens the ego. Like physical pain, it also causes us to tense up, limits our breathing, increases drag, and cuts down power.

Difficulty is the third limiting thought or program. When you're in the middle of a race, thoughts and feelings like "This is hard," "It's impossible," or "I can't do this" reduce power and performance.

The stress and fatigue of a race can express itself like static or snow on a TV set, making it difficult to focus. I asked each rider to select a single power thought that he could tune in to whenever he experienced fear, pain, or difficulty on his mental TV. I asked them to choose a single word that was personally meaningful and that stimulated a good feeling and gave them power. It had to be simple and brief. We wanted a power word that would be comprehensible and useful under pressure.

Each racer selected a different word. Brian, the team's leading racer, chose the word *more*. Whenever he experienced pain, fatigue, self-doubt, or negativity, he would think *more*, turn the wheel, and push a little harder, a little longer, or a little faster. Yvon chose the power word *smooth*. He was a big man who knew that he would often tighten up under pressure and end up having to work harder to accomplish the same result. Chris chose the power word *machine*. He wanted to see himself as inhuman and impervious to pain, doubt, or difficulty. Whenever he noticed himself tuning in to a limiting thought or feeling, Chris would take a breath, draw in energy, turn the wheel, think *machine*, and accelerate. Dave chose the word *fast*. It sparked in him the image to be lighter, tougher, more aggressive, and streamlined. He brought that power word to mind whenever he felt stressed.

Part of their psychological training addressed dealing effectively with the considerable pain, tension, and difficulty produced by their grueling event. I explained to each rider that the natural reaction to pain, tension, and difficulty is to contract, to tighten up, and to try to hold on. Over and over again, I explained to each racer that it is much easier to be aggressive than it is to just "hold on." It's the same in hockey. Holding on changes nothing — it only means that you attempt to ride the race in the state of tension and contraction. And it is much more difficult to be fast and endure in that contracted, limited state.

Along with thinking of being aggressive, we spent a lot of time working with breathing and release (changing channels), so that when a racer felt pain he would use it to focus on breathing, on turning the wheel, and on his or her positive power word.

In the race, the team went out very fast. After 20 kilometers, Chris said he started to feel pain and began to think, "I hurt," followed by, "Just hold on." When he realized what he was thinking, he reminded himself, "It's easier to be aggressive than to hold on," and he went deeper into his breathing, refocused on *machine*, and picked up his pace. Again, about 70 kilometers into the race, Chris said became focused on and locked into pain. Again, the negative thoughts followed. "I can't continue." "Just hold on." Again, he realized what he was doing, refocused on his breathing and on being like a *machine*, and rode right through the pain. He rode a great race. The whole team did.

What makes this story particularly interesting is the bottom line. The riders went out at a fast pace and stayed focused and aggressive throughout the race. Dave, Chris, and Yvon all told me afterward that they were hurting and thought, "I can't do it — I can't go on."

When they noticed themselves tuning in to that feeling or thought, they remembered to go deeper into their breathing, turn the wheel, change channels, generate more power, and refocus on their power word. The end result was they rode the 100 kilometers in 1 hour, 51 minutes, 10 seconds. Their time was an amazing 15 minutes and 30 seconds faster than the previous Canadian record — in fact, it was an unofficial world record in the event.

What's remarkable is that this was not a new team of superstars imported from another part of the planet or the galaxy. Three of the four racers had been part of the team that set the 2:06:40 mark the year before. What was different now was that all the key elements were in place. The right people had been selected, the coaches made sure they knew what to do, and they were in excellent shape. Additionally, they were trained to manage their minds aggressively, to change channels in the face of limiting thoughts and feelings, and to stay tuned in to winning programs — including their power words.[2]

One similarity between hockey and cycling is that in both sports your thoughts and feelings can either enhance or limit your game. Take response-ability to select some positive power thoughts to put on your mental TV. Repeat them often — before, during, and after a game. Repetition builds strength. As your power thinking becomes more of a habit, your on-ice performance will also become consistently better.

Power Statements

In addition to power words and thoughts, you can use a power statement to improve your game.

Al was a talented rushing defenseman. He explained that over the long season there were nights when he felt flat, dull, and unsure of

---

2 For more information, see *Sport Psychology for Cyclists* by Dr. Saul Miller and Peggy Maass Hill (Boulder, Colorado: Velo Press, 1999).

himself and it was a struggle to get up for a game. He asked if there was something he could do to help prepare for the game and be sharper and more positive. First, I showed him how to use his breathing to feel more energized and powerful. Then we reviewed his ABCs and did some mental rehearsal. He visualized himself making all the plays. Lastly, we defined the following "power statement." It consisted of a series of power thoughts and affirmations that reflected the best of Al's play. I encouraged Al to memorize the statement and repeat it to himself before — not during! — each game. I suggested that he take a breath after each thought and see himself performing well. Al was encouraged to do several "reps" of his power statement at a time. Remember, repetition builds strength.

Al's Power Statement

- I am an outstanding hockey player. I am a star.
- I am strong and fast and I read the play well.
- On offense, I have the ability to make things happen.
- I see opportunities and I make excellent passes — to the open man, and on the tape.
- I have a strong, accurate shot.
- I have good wheels. I rush the puck with speed and confidence.
- I am a force when I jump into the play.
- I love to set up and score goals.
- On defense, I am smart and steady.
- I always have good position.
- I keep people to the outside.
- I move people from the front of the net.
- One on one, I am unbeatable.
- I am like a big cat, a tiger. I am quick, strong, and powerful.
- I am intense and focused like a tiger hunting.
- I stay low, head up, eyes open.
- I am quick. I react with my speed and power.
- Offensively and defensively, I am a force.
- I prepare myself well.
- I am a team player.

- I am composed. I don't let criticism bother the tiger, I use it.
- I enjoy playing this game and I am very good at it.
  (Repeat)

The statements you make in your identity statement should make sense to you. They are a combination of your strengths and what you aspire to do. They should be a mix of truths and affirmations (becoming truths). For example, if you have a hard shot and are working to make it more accurate, you could say, "I have a hard, accurate shot." But if you don't skate particularly well it would not be truthful or useful to say, "I have great wheels." It would be more effective to say: "I keep my feet moving. I anticipate the play and react quickly." If you are working on your skating, it makes sense to say, "My foot speed is improving" or "I am getting quicker and faster."

Dennis was a talented young forward, a college star just breaking into the NHL. He had great wheels and soft hands. The rap on Dennis was that at times he simply wasn't aggressive and determined enough. Part of helping him to increase his intensity and follow through was to show him how to use his breathing to pump up and be more centered. Another part of our mental training involved using the following power statement.

- I am an aggressive, hard-working player. I am a star.
- I make things happen.
- I have great wheels.
- I take the puck to the net with speed and confidence.
- I am a scorer. I love to score goals.
- I have good hands.
- I work hard for the puck and I have great finish.
- I have a hard, accurate shot — and I score.
- I have good eyes. I see opportunities and I make excellent passes.
- I am a reliable defensive player.

- I always have good position.
- I am quick and smart.
- I am like a panther hunting — always moving, eyes open, ready to strike.
- I am unstoppable.
- I am physically and mentally ready to play every game.
- I play hard on every shift.
- I am a team player.
- I enjoy playing this game and I am very good at it.
    (Repeat)

Like Al, Dennis was encouraged to repeat each thought in his power statement to himself slowly before games. After each statement he was encouraged to take a breath, see it happening, and then go out on the ice and make it happen.

Exercise 2 ➡

Prepare your own power statement. Write out a statement of who you are (or could be) at your best. Affirm all of your strengths and highlight your potential. If there is a quality you haven't yet manifested, but feel you could, incorporate it into your identity statement. Read this statement to yourself. Repeat it often. Let it become you.

It's important to become aware of who you are and what you need to do to excel. Many players have reported that they found the ABC system and the power statements helpful as focusing tools, and useful components of their pregame preparation. Others have said that the less they think of hockey right before a game, the better they play. Regardless of pregame preferences, everyone can benefit by running positive (instead of negative) programs on their mental TV. The programs you choose are personal. Create and use power thoughts, self-talk, and affirmations that meet your needs and circumstances, and feel right to you.

HOMEWORK ⅲ➡

There are five homework assignments for Chapter 3.

Assignment 1 ⅲ➡

Continue to work with your breathing and feelings of smoothness
and power. Combine breathing and the five-pointed-star image, before
games and when you come off the ice between shifts.

Assignment 2 ⅲ➡

A key factor in your on-ice focus is to have a clear sense of your role
on the ice in a variety of situations. Define your ABCs in each of the
following situations that are relevant to you.

When your team is breaking out of your end:

A. _____

B. _____

C. _____

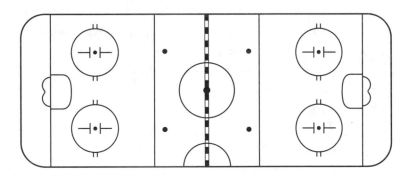

The opposing team picks up the puck and you're playing the transition
game:

A. _____

B. _____

C. _____

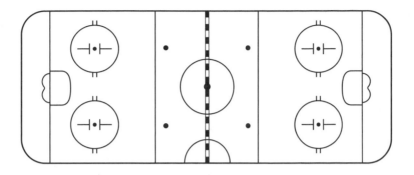

When your team has the puck in its own end:

A. _____

B. _____

C. _____

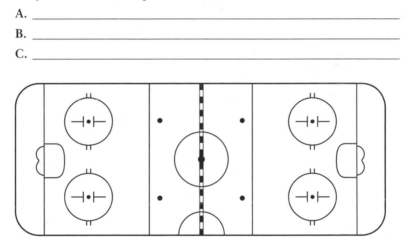

When the opposing team has the puck in your end:

A. _____

B. _____

C. _____

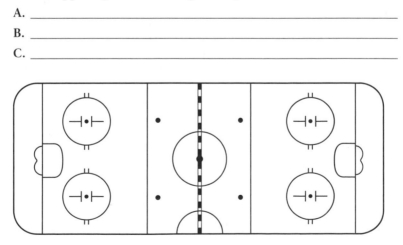

When your team is breaking out/getting the puck out of your end:

A. _____

B. _____

C. _____

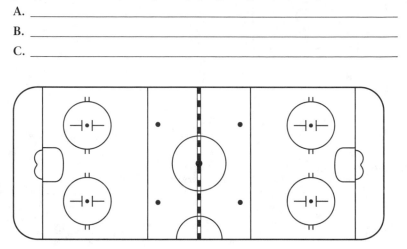

Your forechecking scheme is:

A. _____

B. _____

C. _____

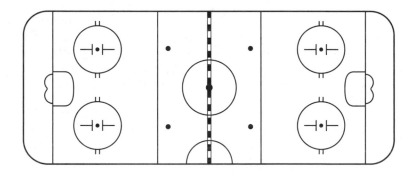

Special Teams

When you are on the power play:

A. _____

B. _____

C. _____

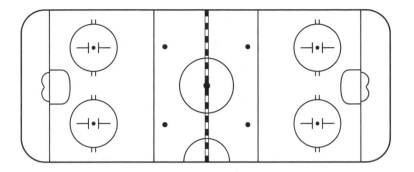

When you are killing a penalty:

A. _____

B. _____

C. _____

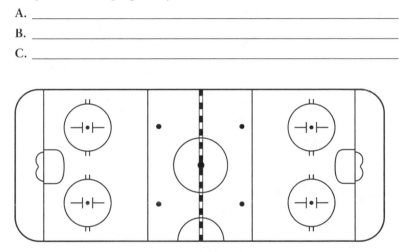

Assignment 3 ➡

Select six to 10 affirmations or power thoughts. Repeat them daily —
in the morning, before stepping out onto the ice, between shifts, and
after a game. Some people tape a list of their favorite affirmations to
the mirror and look at themselves while repeating them. Give it a try.

Assignment 4 [Optional] ➡

Create a power statement that describes you and how you play at
your best. Repeat it to yourself often and imagine yourself performing
at that level.

Assignment 5 (Optional) ➡

We are what we think. There are many books that highlight the power of positive thought, as well as biographies of highly successful athletes and achievers in all walks of life. One way to become a more positive thinker and performer is to become a student of positive thought and read about the impact of positive thinking in the lives of others. Read a positive biography in the next month, then pass it on to a teammate.

Chapter 4

Power Imagery: See It, Do It

When people realize that I'm a sport psychologist, one of the first questions they ask is, "Do you use imagery to help your clients perform better?" I certainly do! Images are the basis of mind, and imagery is basic to high performance. Most of the athletes I work with have used some form of imagery on their own before I even meet them.

Does imagery work? Yes. Research has shown that athletes who mentally rehearse their performance perform significantly better than those who don't. This is particularly true in regard to accuracy. I have worked with athletes in 25 different sports and have seen major-league pitchers, pro golfers, basketball players, and Olympic sharpshooters use imagery rehearsal as an accuracy-enhancing tool. Hockey players can also improve their shooting accuracy and other skills with mental rehearsal.

Longtime NHL coach Mike Keenan says, "The ability to visualize is one of the most valuable psychological abilities a player has to prepare himself to play and improve his performance."

That's not to say imagery training was, or is, the norm. Tiger Williams once told me, "I don't think many guys do it. They may think about wanting to score on the bus on the way to the game, but they don't imagine the actual skating, shooting, and checking that make it happen. And as for coaches teaching it, they don't. At least it never happened to me, and I played for a dozen coaches in the macho pro atmosphere of the NHL."

I hope times are changing. More recently, Chris Pronger, the Norris Trophy–winning captain of the St. Louis Blues, said, "I think most of the players do some visualization. I visualize myself making the plays and doing positive things on the ice. Visualization helps me to get into the right frame of mind."

Essentially, there are four kinds of images I use with hockey players. They are mental rehearsal, imagining the successful end result, stimulating images, and recharging images.

Mental Rehearsal

Mental rehearsal means actually visualizing and practicing in your mind the things you want to do on the ice. That includes your on-ice skills *and* your responses to game situations (ABCs).

Mentally rehearsing on-ice skills includes imagining, seeing, or feeling yourself skating with speed, power, and jump; handling the puck skillfully and with confidence; passing tape to tape; shooting the puck accurately; scoring; and finishing your checks.

To mentally rehearse your response to game situations, you must visualize yourself making good reads and executing your ABCs. In the case of Morris Lukowich, the left-winger we discussed in the last chapter, it's

A. **imagining or seeing himself going into the corner and getting the puck, "like a cat on a mouse."**

   B. imagining himself making a crisp, accurate pass to
      the center in the slot or the man at the (left) point.
   C. experiencing the feeling of snapping a quick, hard,
      accurate wrist shot into the net.

I have suggested to a number of my clients that they score a minimum of 50 goals a day. By that I mean visualize the goal, then imagine yourself shooting a puck into the net — and scoring 50 imaginary goals a day. I even took a photo of a hockey goal, had it blown up to approximately three feet by four feet, and gave the enlargements to members of a team so they could put them on their bedroom walls and use them as the target for their imagery practice. It worked well, except that several players decided to actually shoot pucks at the wall. While that might have improved their on-ice performance, it certainly did not please their landlords.

Brad was an NHL winger who was struggling with scoring. When I visited his home I noticed that he had a lovely large fireplace in his living room. "This is perfect," I said. He looked puzzled. "You should score 50 goals into this fireplace every day. And when you do, pick your corners. Put five in the top left corner. Then five in the top right corner. Then five bottom left. And so on. Sharpen that mental image. Then, when you practice on the ice, you'll see that when you get those two or three scoring opportunities in a game, the puck will start going in for you."

Research suggests that, for the best results, you need to combine your mental rehearsal with on-ice practice. When Terry Crisp was coaching the Soo Greyhounds of the Ontario Hockey League, he mentioned that, just as players practice one-timing a cross-ice pass into the net, he would occasionally have his players run through the same drill without the puck — just imagining the process. He thought it was beneficial.

Exercise 1 ⇒

One of the best ways to begin practicing mental rehearsal is to imagine yourself playing hockey with confidence and impact in a situation in which you have been successful in the past. First, take a couple of breaths. Most of my clients have found that relaxing and breathing improve the quality and clarity of their imagery. Now, see yourself on the ice. Imagine feeling good, skating strongly and smoothly, seeing the whole ice surface, and handling the puck with composure and confidence. Relax, breathe, and experience those feelings.

Begin your imagery with things you do easily. Then gradually imagine performing well in more difficult or challenging aspects of the game. If you are a goalie, see and feel yourself with good position, seeing shots clearly, feeling quick, and handling all shots with confidence. First, imagine a single shooter crossing the blue line and taking a shot. You have good position and handle it easily. Next, imagine the shooter moving in closer to the top of the circle and shooting. Again, you have good position and see the puck clearly and stop it cleanly, without a rebound. Imagine two-on-ones: playing the shooter and making the save, playing the pass and coming across quickly and under control to make the save. Run through a complete warmup in your mind, imagining yourself maintaining good position, being sharp and quick, playing at your best, and making all the saves. If you'll be facing a team with players who have an unusual move or shot, mentally rehearse yourself reacting well and making the save against them.

Repetition builds strength. Repeatedly practicing mental rehearsal will help you develop both your imagination and your on-ice skills so that you will be better able to read, anticipate, and react well in any situation.

Mental rehearsal is useful in all aspects of the game. On offense, imagine yourself skating well, making good passes, jumping up into the play, keeping your feet moving, getting open, going hard to the net, shooting accurately, and scoring. On defense, visualize yourself skating well, reading the play, picking up your check, maintaining good position, angling him to the outside, playing the body, pinning him against the boards, clearing the front of the net, and getting the puck out of your end.

Mentally rehearse your ABCs. Visualize yourself in the offensive zone with the puck, see the breakout, picture yourself coming back hard and angling your check to the boards in transition, and visualize your ABCs on defense, on the power play, and in penalty-killing situations. In each situation, imagine yourself executing the play perfectly.

Don't forget to rehearse difficult situations mentally. It can occasionally be helpful to imagine how you would handle it if things go wrong, if on-ice events happen in a way that you can't control — the referee missing a call, scoring a goal that is disallowed, an unexpected delay in the game, or a change in your role or the line you play on. In each instance, imagine yourself maintaining your composure, taking a breath, staying focused on the positive, and playing good hockey.

Tips for Creating a Winning Hockey Movie

Imagery is like a movie, and you are the director of that movie. Creating and experiencing your own high-performance hockey movies will help you to excel. Here are seven tips that will enhance your mental rehearsal and help you to direct a high-quality experience.

Visualize your ABCs. Uncertainty leads to confusion and nervousness. One way to increase success and reduce stress is to create clear images of your ABCs. Stay tuned into these images. Be specific. Project your energy into the images of what you want to create on the ice.

Relax, then imagine. Whenever possible, release and breathe before putting your imagination to work for you. As you do, the quality of your thoughts and images will become stronger, clearer, and more positive. Take a few minutes before the game to relax, breathe, and imagine performing at your best. In hockey, that may mean being faster, more powerful, being strong on your skates, making good reads, and having soft hands, more patience, and excellent stickhandling, passing, and shooting skills.

Not everybody finds that relaxation enhances their performance. I made a relaxation and imagery tape for Dale, an NHL power forward who wanted to use mental rehearsal to enhance his scoring. When I followed up with him to get his response to the tape, he told me: "I like the imagery part, that helps. But the relaxation makes me too relaxed." My advice to him was to do the imagery alone. Above all, do what works for you.

Stay positive. You get more of what you think about — and what you imagine. Stay focused on the image of you at your best. The only value in running a negative image of something that didn't work — being beaten one-on-one, missing an open net, letting in a soft goal — is to determine what you can do to make that play the next time. Then, mentally rehearse the positive.

Easy first. As a general rule, it's best to move from what's easy to what is more challenging. This is true in mental as well as in physical training. To begin, see and feel yourself handling the simple situations with confidence. In the previous example of a goalie, that could mean starting your mental rehearsal with long shots from the blue line that you see clearly. Then make the imagery more challenging — two-on-ones, breakaways, power-play pressure, and lots of puck movement up close in front of the net.

Be dynamic. Most athletes find their imagery works best if they imagine themselves playing from the perspective of the player on the ice. Others have had success visualizing their performance as if they were a spectator in the stands, watching themselves perform from above. Try both approaches and see what feels and works best.

Similarly, most players find slow-motion imagery very helpful, especially if they're working on moves that demand a lot of skill. But others prefer to mentally rehearse in real time, at full speed.

Be brief. You don't have to imagine an entire shift. You can benefit by imagining five- to 10-second flashes of yourself making a pass, jumping into the play, getting a rebound and finishing, or taking the body and finishing a check.

Use all your senses. Make your mental rehearsal a multi-sensory experience. Most people are strongly visual, so they think that imagery is simply visual. But you may get the best results if you incorporate all the sensory cues: see it, feel it, hear it, and, when appropriate, smell and taste it. For instance, some players have told me they prefer to feel themselves shooting well as opposed to seeing it.

Donald Brashear, an NHL player (a policeman), underlines the importance of mental preparation and specifically mental rehearsal in helping him to maintain control. He said, "The main thing I do to keep control is visualize before the game what's going to happen and how the game is going to unfold. I think about what kind of players they have and which guys are going to be thrown at me. The main thing is anticipation. It's important to anticipate what might be thrown at you so your reactions are natural when you get into the game. That way, when something happens you know what to do right away."

Donald continued, "It's the same with scoring a goal. You imagine you have the puck in a certain type of situation. You visualize it happening . . . and then when it comes to you in the game, your reaction is natural."

I asked Donald about how he deals with different challenges from players mouthing off and trying to get him to fight. How does he keep control? "There are different situations. It depends on the type of player doing it. If it's a tough guy who's bugging me, there's a matter of respect. If he's doing it to me and I don't respond, then I know he's going to be doing it to some other player so I have to take control and show him right away. But if it's a smaller player, I know he's not going to want to drop his gloves. He may be just trying to get me to take a penalty.

"Being in control requires a lot of focus — a lot of work with your mind just before the game, and also the day before the game. I think about it a lot. You also have to consider the circumstance in the game, who's winning and does your team need a lift? I have started fights at times when it woke up the other team and gave *them* a lift. Obviously, that's not good. So you have to consider many things, go over it in your mind, and prepare yourself well in advance."

There is no one right time or way to do mental rehearsal. Some players do it the night before a game, some the afternoon of a game, some a few minutes before a game, and some not at all. Some players use images that relate directly to them playing against the team they are going to face in an upcoming game. For others, mental rehearsal is more generic and focuses on making plays regardless of the opposition. Experiment and discover what works best for you.

Imagining the Successful End Result

A second kind of imagery that you can incorporate into your hockey preparation is to think of the successful end result you want to create. Create and hold the image of exactly what it is that you are working toward, whether it's making the team, making the play-offs, or winning a championship.

Most sport psychologists believe that it's more important to think of the *process* of how you are going to get there — that is, mental rehearsal — than it is to focus on the end result. I agree. However, having a clear end result in mind can mobilize a process that puts powerful unconscious forces to work for you. It can also sustain you and help you to endure the rigors of training that are necessary to get you where you want to go.

Visualizing yourself playing in the NHL, on a national team, or at the major junior, college, school, or rep level, is an image that may help you to sustain the drive you need to reach your goal. Putting a photograph on the wall of yourself (or a favorite player or role model) scoring or making a big save, or being a part of a team that you aspire to, can support you. A success image is no substitute for expending the effort necessary to succeed, but it can help you to reach that goal.

Exercise 2 ⇒

Pick an end result and put a picture of it up on the wall. Use the picture to remind yourself of what you are working to achieve and why the training and consistent effort that you put out are important. Let that image become a source of energy to support you in maintaining your efforts.

Stimulating Images

The third kind of imagery I use to help athletes to excel is one that some hockey players have found useful — and that many have found fun. I often ask the question, "If you had to pick an animal that would give you qualities you want to have on the ice, and that would help you to play winning hockey, which animal would you choose?" The animals that most hockey players select are the big cats — the tigers, lions, leopards, jaguars, and panthers. Some defenseman have picked bears.

The idea is that each of us is a combination of an animal — with a strong, powerful physical body, as well as strong, powerful emotions and instincts — and an angel. The part of our being that is an angel enables us to use our thoughts and images to create and shape our reality. The animal part relates to our emotion, heart, physical strength, and energy.

You can use imagery to awaken the animal spirit within you. The thing about the big cats is that they have tremendous power, as well as balance and speed. They are brave and aggressive. They are crafty and smart. They play their angles perfectly. They love to hunt and they never worry. If they return from hunting without their prey, they don't sulk or ruminate about it. And unlike some hockey players I have known, they don't run themselves down or get depressed if they have a poor shift or if they haven't scored in a couple of games.

Bret Hedican is one of the most mobile defensemen in the NHL. He is also a very motivated athlete and an excellent team player who was willing to explore how sport psychology training could enhance his game. Bret says that what helped him most in our early sessions was to learn how to relax and stay composed. In wanting to play well he would sometimes try too hard, which of course could be counterproductive.

After mastering relaxation and breathing, one of the things that helped him most was imagery, specifically the image of a jaguar. "Sometimes I imagine myself as a jaguar," he says, "hunting, being low on the ice, having good vision, knowing who's on the ice and where they are, and being ready to react quickly."

Bret went on to say, "I think of myself as a jaguar unaffected by stresses and negatives, by good shifts or bad shifts, or the press. If we have back-to-back games and I'm tired, I hunt smarter. I have learned to assess my energy level. And when I'm tired, like an animal, I use my energy better. I'm wiser and more patient. I stay back in the weeds a little more when I'm hunting."

Your animal image should represent you at your best. It's you at your physically strongest, with reflexes sharp, quick to react, great balance, power, and jump. By selecting the tiger or panther, you can identify with a power source with great courage and heart, with superhuman quickness and speed, with strength, power, and remarkable reflexes, that can attack and hunt with efficiency. Animal images can provide power and heart.

When you think of a cheetah, tiger, jaguar, or whatever animal image you choose, allow it to awaken that animal in you. Allow it to stimulate you to turn the wheel. Turning the wheel fires up the tiger. It awakens your speed and jump and power.

As I mentioned, several defensemen have selected bears rather than one of the big cats. When I asked Jeff, a veteran of the NHL and the International Hockey League, what appealed to him about being a bear, he pointed to two qualities: size and power. He described how, as a bear, he could visualize himself going into the corner and overpowering his man, or becoming an immovable force in front of the net. He reminded me that bears are not only strong, but they're also very quick. Several wingers (and they weren't all from the University of Michigan) chose wolverines because of their aggressiveness and tenacity.

One NHL defenseman, with whom I consulted for many years, asked me to help him sharpen his focus and intensity. I found him living in a very comfortable, luxurious home, quite removed from the sparse, spartan surroundings that had nurtured his competitive spirit years before in his junior hockey days, when we had first met. I reminded him that, to reawaken that animal spirit, he should use his breathing to turn the wheel and fire up the lion. Then I suggested, half jokingly, that he might stimulate that animal intensity in his game if he were to give up his soft lifestyle and extracurricular distractions and go sleep in the backyard.

If you are going to use animal imagery and call on the energy and spirit that are there, you have to do the training necessary to support it.

Exercise 3 ➠

Select the image of an animal that appeals to you. Think about turning the wheel, generating power, and firing up that animal. Whether you are under pressure, tired, and have low energy, or are dominating, use the situation you are in to stimulate you to turn the wheel and energize the animal, then think about the ABCs or about "hunting."

Recharging Images

Hockey is a physically and mentally demanding game. On the ice, players are expected to give 100 percent. Off the ice, you should have a way to recharge, something I'll discuss in greater depth in Chapter 12. However, there are two kinds of recharging imagery that I use and I want to describe here.

Recharging image number one involves imagining a safe, comfortable, high-energy place where you can rest, recharge, and get ready to do battle. Many people use images from nature to recharge. Some imagine being at the beach, relaxing and feeling the warm sun on their bodies, hearing the waves rolling in, breathing in the sea air. Others imagine being on a mountaintop where they can see for miles around, breathing the clear, fresh, mountain air and feeling powerful. Still others are at peace in the woods, by a small lake — calm, quiet, breathing easily, resting deeply. Some choose to imagine being in their bedrooms at home, where they are comfortable and secure in bed, with no disturbances or distractions — a safe, familiar place where they can rest deeply.

The value of these images is that they provide a supportive context that will help you to relax and recharge wherever you are. Whether you're on a bus or plane or in a hotel room far away from home, all you have to do is close your eyes and think of your special place and that image will help you to rest and recharge.

Another way to use imagery to recharge is to relax, breathe, and imagine (as we did in Chapter 2) that you have a personal connection to an unlimited supply of energy. As you breathe, allow energy to flow to you and through you. If any part of your body feels tired or sore, imagine that you are breathing more energy or oxygen into that part of your body. You can use the star image we discussed earlier and combine this recharging image with the imagery of being in one of the special relaxing spaces I described above. During the season, I suggest a 20-minute recharging session each day.

Experiment with high-performance imagery until you become an expert. As always, assess and adjust, and develop images that work for you. Combining imagery with right feelings and power thoughts is very effective. Imagery can be a powerful aid to your preparation and on-ice performance. You can also use it to help develop a more positive, high-performance attitude.

Use Video to Program Your Mental TV

Video can enhance your imagery — and your play. Many teams have a coach who analyzes video of games and breaks it down so that players can use it to prepare for games and develop their skills. I have also seen coaches tape practices and then review how well a player has executed the drills. Video is an excellent training tool. When you have seen what has to be done, it's easier to replicate it. Similarly, if you are able to see what you are doing wrong, you'll find it easier to correct.

I have suggested to many players that they create a four- to five-minute video highlight tape of themselves playing at their best. A forward's video might show him on offense, skating well, with speed and jump, taking a pass, going hard to the net, scoring, winning the puck on the boards, making good passes, and jumping into the play and going to the net. On defense it could show him working hard, being an aggressive forechecker, skating back, having good position, and covering his check.

Watching a positive performance video can strengthen your perception of your play and add to your confidence. It can also provide high-quality, high-performance images for your mental rehearsal. Remember, repetition builds strength, so watch your video often.

Some players have inserted clips of tigers and panthers hunting into their performance tapes to create stimulating videos that puts them in a more competitive frame of mind. Others have added music. It can all work. Be creative. Developing players and veterans alike have also found it beneficial to watch the tapes of other players — both for pregame preparation and so that they can see positive role models performing well.

Paul Kariya of the Mighty Ducks of Anaheim says he uses imagery more in conjunction with practice than pregame preparation. He said he also uses video, especially to prepare against teams that he doesn't see very often. "We play Dallas and Los Angeles eight times a year. I know what to expect against them. I have found video to be especially helpful in preparing to play against the teams we only meet one or twice a year, to review their tendencies and weaknesses."

Some coaches use video as a motivational tool. Several teams I've worked with have made highlight tapes for the playoffs that feature some of the team's outstanding plays blended with music and crowd reactions. The idea is to get players excited about the challenge. It's an effective technique. One important note: coaches who do this should be aware of the range of personality differences of their players (I'll say more about this in Chapter 7), because what lifts some players to their optimum level arousal may get others too pumped up.

So far I've mentioned that performance images should be positive. It's the same with video. However, it can be useful to view poor play in order to clarify and eliminate mistakes. Once the mistakes are understood, however, focus on positive images.

Motivational highlight tapes usually emphasize a team's best plays. However, there are instances when it can be beneficial to highlight the opposition's fallibility. I made that recommendation to one coach during the playoffs when his team was facing an opponent that had dominated them all season long. In such a case, it can be helpful to show the opposition's vulnerability. Highlight them making mistakes, being caught out of position, missing checks, and getting knocked around, scored on, and allowing soft goals.

Similarly, facing an opponent with a hot goalie can cause some players to become uptight, negative, and discouraged. Video is one way to remedy the thinking that "He can't be beaten." I once advised an NHL coach to prepare a tape showing Dominik Hasek, the goalie they were to face in the next playoff round, being scored on repeatedly.

One point to be aware of, however, is that these "negative highlight tapes" should be accompanied by a reminder that our success is about our response-ability to play winning hockey.

As a coach, when you use video as a teaching aid, remember also that the desired behavior should be clearly defined. Roger Neilson is an expert at using the telestrator to show players exactly what he is looking for on the ice. "This gap is too big," he'll say. "This gap is just right. Keep your stick on him here. That's perfect. Take that angle away."

If you are a coach, be clear about what you want to communicate with video. If players see what's desired, they can internalize the images into their mental rehearsal. Don't assume that everyone will appreciate what you've seen. One client, who was an NHL veteran, was given a game video by his coach and told in a critical manner to take it home and watch it. He did, and couldn't find anything wrong with his play. As a matter of fact, he told me, "I didn't realize that I played so well. I don't know what the hell he's talking about."

It is not a good idea to use video as a punishment. One NHL coach who was angry with his team's disappointing performance in a game told the players to come in at 8:00 the next morning. When they arrived, he cued up the video of the previous night's game, said, "Watch this!" and stormed out of the room. One of the players told me: "It was real early. Half the team was dozing off and hardly anyone really watched the tape." If anything, the exercise was a turn-off, not a turn-on. Indeed, it might have contributed to the players' being less attentive viewers in the future.

HOMEWORK Ⅲ➡

There are six homework assignments for Chapter 4.

Assignment 1 Ⅲ➡

Continue to work with your power words this week. Combine them with your breathing. See if you can get your words to evoke a performance-enhancing feeling and create a performance-enhancing image. Incorporate them into your game. Continue to work with your affirmations. Select your six favorite power thoughts. Repeat them often.

Assignments 2, 3, and 4 Ⅲ➡

There are three kinds of high-performance imagery to work with this week: mental rehearsal, imagining the successful end result, and stimulating imagery.

There are two ways to practice mental rehearsal. First, after relaxing and breathing, see yourself playing with confidence and ease. Visualize yourself handling the puck well and skating well, with good eyes and making good reads. Run through your offensive and defensive ABCs. Second, imagine varying your intensity, first energizing and "attacking," then calming and "smoothing."

To create the image of a successful end result, choose an objective that you want to achieve. (It is important to have an idea of what you are striving for.) Put a picture or drawing that represents that image up on your wall, or somewhere else where you can see it. Put that image in your mind. Clarifying your intentions is very empowering. Reflecting on that image can give you energy to carry on and can help you realize your goal or dream. Every once in a while, sit back and imagine yourself having achieved that goal.

Finally, think of an animal that gives you the qualities you want to bring to your game. Pick an animal that appeals to you and that you find stimulating. The big cats are especially popular because of their speed, balance, quickness, power, and beauty. Choose an image that works for you. Allow yourself to experience an awakening of your animal instinct. It can stimulate your hockey. Work hard and have fun.

Assignment 5 ⇒

Continue to work with your breathing and relaxation on a daily basis, both in preparation for a game and for practice. Combine your daily breathing sessions with some recharging imagery. Some players find it very beneficial to run this process a couple of hours before a game. Others find that it makes them feel too relaxed and prefer to recharge the night before a game. Find out what works best for you.

Assignment 6 ⇒

Study a video of one of your recent games. Look for things you do well and acknowledge them to yourself. Look for things you can improve and practice making that happen. From time to time, do a video review of your play.

If you can, make a two- to four-minute highlight video of yourself playing well, both offensively and defensively.

Chapter 5

A Winning Hockey Attitude

A winning attitude is a way of thinking that predisposes you toward being more successful. With a winning attitude, almost anything is possible. And attitude is a matter of choice.

During a meeting with a championship-caliber junior hockey team, I asked the players, "What contributes to a winning attitude?"

"Being positive," one player answered. When I asked him to be more specific, he said, "Thinking positive thoughts. Knowing what you want to do and thinking you can do it."

We had been working with imagery, so another player said, "It's having positive images, like seeing yourself playing well and saying positive things to yourself."

"What else?" I asked the group. The answers came fast.

"A winning attitude is about being motivated."

"Working hard for what you want."

"Confidence is part of a winning attitude."

"So is pride."

"Mental toughness."

"Expectation."

"Self-esteem."

"You're all right," I chimed in. "Many qualities make up a winning attitude."

Let's spend a few minutes talking about what we can do to strengthen some of these winning qualities.

Commitment

Success begins with motivation. Motivation is what moves us to action. It is about desire, goals — and commitment. As I said at the outset of the book, goals work. Setting goals can clarify direction and increase success. But setting goals and repeating your goal statement doesn't guarantee success. You still have to do the work. Some players set excellent goals for themselves but are simply not willing to follow through with the day-to-day action necessary to make their goals a reality. Commitment is the willingness to do what's necessary to get the result you want.

Your commitment is a reflection of your motivation. If your goal is to get to the top of the mountain, the way up is one step at a time, rain or shine. Taking the time, spending the energy, and making it happen are what commitment is about. In hockey, one step at a time means doing the day-to-day physical and mental training needed to build up the fitness base, skill sets, productive focus, emotional control, and positive attitude required to excel. It's making yourself more response-able.

Consistent hard work is an expression of commitment. Even the top players know the value of hard work. When I asked Pavel Bure what advice he could offer a young player wanting to develop his scoring ability, he said, "The only advice I have is general. Work hard." And Wayne Gretzky, the perennial NHL all-star and Hall of Famer, has said: "I'm gifted, but I've worked hard for everything I've gotten. Gordie Howe and Bobby Orr worked hard, too. Like them, I didn't say, 'I'm gifted. I don't have to work hard anymore.'"[1]

Again, commitment is the willingness to put in the necessary time and effort to excel. "Willingness" means you make the choice. From a mental training point of view, it goes back to a principle that we discussed in Chapter 1: Whatever comes up, use it. Either you use it, or it uses you. If you are genuinely committed to being the best you can be, then it's important to learn how to use whatever situation, challenge, or obstacle is confronting you.

The process of "using it" involves clearing the screen on your mental TV and refocusing on the positive. When people are presented with a challenging stimulus, their initial response is often an automatic impulse to contract. Using it is about activating the release reflex — releasing (whether it's tension, negativity, or anxiety), breathing in energy and power, and refocusing on the positive, on what you want to do on the ice, on your ABCs, on being a star, a scorer, a winner, or a tiger.

Cliff was the center on a line that had scored close to 100 goals during the NHL regular season. Just before the playoffs he was switched to a line with two hard-working checkers as his wingers. At first he was upset with the change. He saw himself as a scorer and set-up man and he wondered, "How can I play with these guys?" Obviously, he had no control over the line change. But what he *could* control was his reaction to it. I asked him, "How can you use it?" When he didn't respond, I said, "You've been seen as a one-dimensional player, an offensive guy. Here's an opportunity to develop your complete game. This new line can become an excellent checking line, and when life gives you lemons it's best to make lemonade." He accepted the challenge, changed his focus, and used it to become a more complete player. All the way to the finals, he played winning hockey, and the line he centered was acknowledged as the team's best throughout the playoffs.

---

1 Quoted in *The Edge: The Guide to Fulfilling Dreams, Maximizing Success and Enjoying a Lifetime of Achievement*, edited by Howard Ferguson (Cleveland: Getting the Edge Co., 1990).

Winners are not free from disappointment, fear, and negativity. Like everyone else, they experience uncertainty and doubt. It's just that they don't dwell on it. Instead, they use it to refocus and stay on the power channel. Winners use everything.

On a visit to Sault Ste. Marie, Ontario, a few years ago I met with Harry Wolfe, the voice of the Soo Greyhounds for more than four decades. As we spoke, Harry pointed out two NHL prospects playing with the Greyhounds. He said that both had been at NHL training camps and both had been sent back to the junior team. There was, however, a huge difference between the two.

One of the players was sulking about being returned him to his junior team. He thought he shouldn't have been sent down, that the big-league team hadn't given him a fair chance. Since his return, he was negative, full of complaints, and playing poorly. The other player had a completely different spin on his experience at the NHL camp. He said, "What I realized is that I can play up there. I'm good enough. It was great and I'm going back." Since being sent back to junior he was working hard and playing very well. Which of the two players do you think made it back to the NHL? If you picked the second one, you're right. The second player used his experience, while the first one let it use him. Remember, attitude is a matter of choice, and winners use everything.

Whether you are a player or a coach, set a standard of commitment for yourself and model a standard of commitment for your team-mates. Become more aware of what's happening around you, and whatever it is, choose to use it.

I've spoken to many parents about their sons' and daughters' development as hockey players. One father I know gave his 16-year-old son, an NHL prospect, some very sound advice when the young man left home to play in the Western Hockey League. He told his son that most of the players on the team were not going to go any further up the hockey ladder than the major junior level they were currently playing at. He said, "If you're motivated and committed to going beyond that level, then don't just be 'one of the guys.' Involve yourself and emulate the work habits of the players on your team who are winners, who share a motivation and commitment to develop their abilities, to go further, and to be the best they can be."

It's good advice. Scotty Bowman said the same thing when I asked him about commitment and developing potential: "If you want to improve at something, anything, get involved with people or players who are better than you. Then you'll get better."

Hockey is a team game. As much as you may be focused and try to avoid hassles, it's not always easy to get along with all your teammates and coaches. Karen was a dedicated young junior player. We had been discussing her goals and her commitment when she complained about a self-centered teammate who was making her life miserable.

"She really bugs me," Karen said. "She's selfish. All she thinks about is herself, on and off the ice. But I know I have to get along with her. Do you have any suggestions?"

I suggested to Karen that this player was giving her a refocusing opportunity and if she was really committed to being the best she could be, she could — and should — use the situation rather than allow it to use her.

"How do I do that?"

"First, I would try talking to her," I replied.

"Impossible," she said. "I've tried half a dozen times. She's a jerk."

"Then I suggest that every time you notice her behaving like a jerk, you take a breath and clear your stress off the screen. And instead of getting upset, see yourself making a pass, putting the puck in the net, or dishing out a hard check. Say to yourself, 'I'm focused, and nothing can get me off track.' If she bugs you 10 times during a practice, that's an opportunity to do 10 positive reps of yourself playing well."

Adapting something that Goethe, the great writer and philosopher, is alleged to have said, I say, "If it doesn't kill you, use it to make you stronger."

Exercise 1 ⟶

Define your commitment. Review your hockey goals. What are your long- and short-term goals, for you individually? For your team? What's your commitment? What price are you willing to pay to achieve your goals?

Now pick one thing about your game that has been "using you" and getting you down and think of how you can use it to be a more effective player.

Confidence

Confidence is another key to a winning attitude. Confidence has to do with how we see ourselves. If someone is confident, they believe they can do the job, and that belief makes it more likely the job will get done. An important question for most athletes is "How do I grow my confidence? How do I transform doubt and negativity into that confident sense of being a winner?"

I think there are two basic ways to build confidence. Late one evening I got a phone call from an NHL coach who was aboard the team plane heading home following a disappointing loss. The team had been losing consistently, and this particular defeat was just too much.

The coach wanted me to speak to his players the next day about confidence. When I entered the room, the players were already assembled. I was introduced and I began by asking, "What builds confidence?" The room was silent.

Finally one player — the captain — said, "Winning."

Of course, he was right. The most basic way to build confidence is to experience success. Success leads to more success. Success in the form of winning and scoring grows confidence. However, confidence is fragile. If you are a scorer and you haven't been scoring, you can begin to feel anxious and self-doubt can creep into your thinking. Scoring erases the self-doubt. If a team has been losing repeatedly and blowing leads, their thinking can become negative; they will begin to anticipate failure — "Oh, no, it's happening again" or "There's no way" — and confidence disappears. Win a game or two and the players begin to think more positively and more confidently.

Markus Naslund, the captain of the Vancouver Canucks, made an interesting comment about scoring and confidence. Markus said, "When I am playing well and scoring goals, I really look forward to every shift. I think positive. I think and feel like I can score every time I get on the ice. When I haven't scored in several games, I notice that I start thinking more negatively. Thoughts like, 'How long will this scoring drought last?' start creeping into my mind." These thoughts vanish soon after he scores a goal or two. The experience Markus describes is common. After people have performed well they feel more confident, and that influences their play positively. The trick is to learn how to create those confident feelings *before* the result, so as to increase the likelihood of the result happening.

John was a scorer. He had been a scorer and an all-star in junior hockey and led his team to a national championship. That success had carried over when he began his pro career. But one day John telephoned and said, "I'm in a slump. Since the all-star game [two weeks before], I haven't been able to score and my confidence is gone." He asked me if I could help him regain his confidence and his scoring touch.

I listened to him, took a breath, and replied, "John, you're a scorer. Scorers sometimes have periods when they score less. If you're worried about it, I'll recommend a few things you can do to start scoring again. The first thing is to remember to relax and breathe."

"I'm doing that," he replied. "I do it in the afternoon before a game. And I focus on my breathing when I'm waiting to go on the ice, just before the start of each period."

So far, so good. "The second thing," I told him, "is mental rehearsal. It's helpful to visualize scoring goals the way you can, in every possible way. Imagine working hard, going hard to the net, and scoring. Imagine yourself one-timing a pass and scoring. Imagine scoring from the slot. Imagine jumping on a rebound and popping it in. Imagine scoring on a good shot. Imagine scoring in the top corner, bottom corner, and five-hole. Imagine deflecting a shot into the goal. Imagine someone banking one in off your back or your bottom into the net. Imagine yourself scoring goals and having fun. I want you to score 50 imaginary goals twice a day. Do you know what I mean?"

John said he knew what I meant and that he would do some positive imagery. "Remember," I added, "every time you have a negative or worrisome thought, take a breath and picture yourself scoring a goal."

The third thing I told John to do to sharpen his goal-scoring reflex was to practice. Practice moving the puck with his linemates. Practice his shot. Practice one-timing a pass. Practice tip-ins. "Practice does make perfect," I reminded him.

"The fourth thing to remember, John — and it's important to know this in your bones and say it to yourself again and again — is 'I am a good hockey player. I am good at generating chances and putting the puck in the net. I am a scorer. That's who I am. I love to play hockey. I love to work hard. I love to score goals.'

"Follow this advice, John, and the goals will happen."

When I spoke to him a week later, the drought was over and he was scoring again.

The number one answer to the question of what builds confidence is success. Success, winning, scoring, and shutting down the opposition all lead to confidence. But what if you haven't had success lately, or at this level? What can you do to grow your confidence when you haven't been winning or scoring? The answer lies in preparation.

To return to the mountain analogy in the previous chapter, if you look up from the valley to the top of a high mountain peak, the task of climbing the mountain may seem overwhelming. You may lack the confidence and belief that you can do it. However, it becomes easier to envision if you break the climb into steps and stages, with many steps constituting a stage. If you know from your training that you can take these steps and complete each stage, your confidence that you can complete the climb will grow.

In climbing your hockey mountain, see yourself doing what's necessary and taking the steps to build your strength, skills, fitness, and ability to read the game. Approach your development in steps and stages. Break the challenge down into manageable steps and do what's necessary.

Regaining your confidence and returning to top form after an injury requires the same approach. Set a long-term goal and some attainable in-between goals. See yourself doing the basics and performing well at each stage. As you do, your belief in your ability will grow. You'll know that you can do it. Just as I advised John, see yourself doing it with mental rehearsal, and then actually do it in practice. Then, finally, make it or allow it to happen in game situations. Two affirmations that are relevant and worth repeating are, "My mind is a force I use to make things happen" and "Self-love is allowing myself to win."

Corey was an outstanding college player and an all-star defenseman in the American Hockey League. He had been called up to the NHL several times, but never seemed to stick for very long. When I met him he was playing well in the AHL. He was both a defensive and offensive force for his team and a "go-to guy" on the power play. I acknowledged his play.

As we spoke, he mentioned how much he wanted another shot in the NHL. Shortly after our meeting, Corey was given that opportunity and I watched him in his first few games back in the NHL. Initially, he seemed tentative, cautious, and overly conservative. I told him so. He explained that he was very confident in the minors, where he had the green light from the coach to take chances, rush, shoot the puck — whatever he thought would work. But at the NHL level he was afraid of making a mistake.

I told Corey that the way he'd been playing in the minors was the very reason the big-league club had called him up — he was the guy who could make the plays. "While I understand your concern about making a mistake," I told him, "if you play a tentative, 'watch out' game, you're not showing them who you can be — and you may not be around very long."

Corey appreciated the feedback. It reminded him to be himself. To build his confidence I encouraged him to use his anxiety to visualize himself as the take-charge guy he was capable of being and to play that way. As he became more aggressive, he had more of an impact — and more fun.

Playing good defense is a daunting task. However, as you break the challenge down into the various elements, what has to be done becomes clearer and seems more possible. To excel on defense is a matter of developing the following skills:

- **Skating**
- **Reading the game**
- **Maintaining good position**
- **Playing strongly without the puck**
- **Clearing the front of the net**
- **Playing against size**
- **Handling the puck**
- **Playing against speed**
- **Gapping up**
- **Getting the puck out of our end**
- **Passing on the tape**
- **Controlling the puck at the point**
- **Shooting from the point**

To build confidence, mentally rehearse each of these elements, then practice them on the ice, until you feel "I can handle this." Then move on to the next challenging part of your game. Work consistently with focus, feeling, and commitment until gradually you have the sense that "I can do it."

Practice the things you have to work on to be a better player. Practice with imagery. Practice on the ice. Practice in practice. Practice until you know you can. "I am strong on my skates. My skating continues to improve. I read the play well. I gap up. I play the body. I always have good position. I keep my man to the outside. I pin him on the boards. I take his stick away. I clear the front of the net. I get the puck out of our end. I make good outlet passes. I jump into the play. I am comfortable and effective at the point. I make good reads and good passes. I shoot hard and with accuracy. I am in control." As you practice these elements and see your ability grow in each area, your performance and self-image as a competent defenseman will improve — and your confidence will grow.

Chain together the elements in your mental rehearsal. See yourself breaking up a play in your end, handling the puck with composure, and jumping up into the play. As you do, you will gradually sense and "know" that you have what it takes to play good defense in any situation you may encounter in any game. As you practice, your confidence will grow and you will look at any situation or opponent and say to yourself, "I can handle it (or them)."

Nobody is perfect. Remember, whenever you experience a poor shift (for instance, if you are a defenseman and you are caught out of position and get beaten; if you are a scorer and you miss the open net; if you are a goalie and you allow a soft goal), use it. Think of what you can do to improve your performance next time. Frame your efforts in a positive light. As you do, feel your confidence grow.

In Chapter 3 I described how Morris Lukowich used his ABCs (plus breathing and imagery) to improve his power-play performance. Years later, when I discussed the experience with Morris, he said, "What we did really helped me to rebuild my confidence. You helped me to structure a plan and then get my mind uncluttered so I could refocus on executing that plan. I had all this other stuff in my head and I was starting to worry. I knew I could do it but the question was how? You helped me unravel the clutter and put together a how-to plan so all my energies could go into doing it instead of being confused about what to do. Once I got past that, I started to believe, 'Yes, I can,' and then I began to play better."

Exercise 2 ⟶

Design your own confidence-building training program. Assess and adjust. Identify some parts of your game that challenge you, where you feel your confidence is limited. Think about the elements you would have to improve on to perform more effectively. Think about what you would have to do to really master these elements. What on-ice practice would improve your confidence in these areas? What self-talk and imagery would help? Exercise your commitment and do the practice. Preparation builds confidence. See yourself practicing and improving.

The easiest answer to the question "How do I build my confidence?" is simply "Improve your preparation and change your focus."

- Magic happens when you set small, incremental goals.
- Make a commitment.
- Work consistently.
- Run positive programs.
- Mentally rehearse things.
- Think power thoughts.
- Keep moving forward. Take steps. Complete stages.
- Say positive things to yourself.
- Acknowledge yourself for improving on each element or stage.
- Use your unsuccessful experiences to make you better.
- Use your successful experiences to grow your confidence.
- Then, move on to the next element.
- Chain the elements together.
- Run positive programs; engage in positive self-talk and imagery.

I spent several years working with the Los Angeles Rams of the National Football League. In football, the field-goal kicker has one of the most pressure-filled jobs on the team. A kicker's performance can be affected by confidence. At each practice, the Rams' kicker employed an interesting technique to build his confidence. He would start out by kicking short field goals — first, from the 10-

yard line. After making two or three kicks in a row he would move back to the 15-yard line. When he was successful at that distance, he would move back to the 20, the 25, the 30, and so on. As he progressed though this routine he strengthened his confidence — as well as his identity of himself as a competent kicker.

The point I want to reiterate — and one I've observed in every sport, including hockey — is that confidence flows from preparation and success. Do the necessary work to experience success in the elements and steps en route to your ultimate goal and your confidence will grow. Growing your successes and your confidence is directly related to improving the quality of your mental preparation.

Deserving Success

Another facet of a winning hockey attitude is what I call a sense of deserving. Deserving relates to confidence. Confronted with a goal-scoring opportunity, some players just go for it. It's as if they feel that they deserve to score, and they're going to take the opportunity. Most scorers have this quality. Others don't feel as confident or deserving. It's as though they don't expect success, or they need permission to go for it. Sometimes it appears that they think too much.

Deserving is an attitude. It's believing that you deserve to express all your ability. The opportunity is there and it's yours. There's no holding back. Remember, if you don't believe you deserve it, it's unlikely you're going to make it happen. What I have found useful in helping athletes who don't feel deserving or confident about their ability in a particular situation is having them go back to feeling empowered and build step by step from there.

Exercise 3 ➡

If deserving is an issue for you, here's a three-step process you might use to increase your sense of deserving.

Sit back and tune in to your breathing rhythm. Give yourself time for the breath to come in, and to go out. As you do, remind yourself that you deserve your time. I'm not just talking about understanding a concept, but actually experiencing a feeling. As you begin to experience time in your breathing rhythm, know that you deserve your time.

Imagine being on the ice. Imagine skating well, with ease, speed, and power. As you do, affirm that you deserve to express your ability — *all* your ability. Know and feel that you deserve to express your ability.

Bring that awareness and sense of deserving to a game situation. If you find yourself in a game with more experienced players, or up against teams that have outplayed you in the past, and if you start to feel less than powerful and less "deserving" than they are, use this dis-ease to go deeper into your breathing and acknowledge what you know to be true: "I deserve my time" and "I deserve to express my ability." Then, bring that sense of deserving into the game.

Something I often say to young players to remind them of their sense of deserving is "It's your puck. Play like it's your puck."

One team I worked with always seemed to play better when they were down by a goal or two. They rarely established a lead and held it. It was as if they didn't believe they deserved to win. However, they were clear that they didn't deserve to lose. So when they were losing they worked hard (and with a sense of deserving) to battle back. Unfortunately, they weren't a good enough team that they could afford to spot the opposition a goal or two. To win, they needed a change of attitude.

Identity

Identity is another ingredient in a winning attitude. Your identity is who you think and feel you are — and, to a lesser extent, it's who others perceive you to be. For most of us, our identity evolves with time and life experience. Most successful athletes have some identity of themselves as an effective competitor. Your hockey identity can be a determinant of how you behave and perform as a player. Most important, it's something you can shape and control. As I've said before, you get more of what you think about. If you think you can, you may. If you think you can't, you won't. The way you talk to yourself and visualize yourself performing well are two important determinants of your identity and self-image. Your hockey identity can give you the energy and confidence that will lift you to excel, or it can act like a weight to slow you down, tire you, and limit you from expressing your potential.

Doug Risebrough, the general manager of the Minnesoota Wild, tells a story from his playing days with the Montreal Canadiens. The Habs, a perennial NHL powerhouse, were playing an expansion team, one to which they had never lost a game. At the end of the second period in the Montreal Forum, the Canadiens were losing by three goals. In the dressing room, surrounded by mementos of past Canadiens championship teams, the players were angry with their on-ice performance — or lack thereof. Doug says the mood in the dressing room was "That's not who we are. We're not the kind of team to lose to these bums." The Canadiens stormed back onto the ice and scored three goals in the third period.

I got a call from the coach of an AHL team. His team had won its division in the regular season, but was beaten decisively by a sixth-place team in the first game of the playoffs. "We played poorly," the coach said. He was concerned and asked for a suggestion on how to refocus the team.

I asked him what he meant when he said the team had played poorly. Exactly what did the players do in last night's game that was different from what they had been doing all year long?

"We were tight," he replied. "We were forcing everything. We didn't play smart. We were too aggressive. We didn't stay high on the forecheck. We pinched and got caught. And we chased the puck." He had a theory as to why the team had reacted the way it had and he wondered if it would be a good idea to discuss it with the players.

"Keep it simple," I told him. "Focus on their identity — remind them who they are. Show them some video highlights of last night's poor performance and say, 'That's not acceptable and that's not who we are.' Encourage them to play smart, to remember their ABCs. *Then* show them some video highlights in which they're playing exemplary hockey and tell them, 'That's who we are. All year long we prided ourselves on being smart and working hard. That's who we are. If we play like that, we'll win.'"

Scotty Bowman says that a team's identity is one of the most important ingredients in winning. It's true. An identity image of who you are and how you can — and should — perform can move you to do things you think yourself physically incapable of doing. The same is true of a team. Conversely, wearing the identity or self-image of "loser" or "choke artist" can be limiting. Our identity can lift us to super performances or slow us down and limit us.

Identity is not a static entity. It is something that is formed over time and by experience and it can be reshaped. You can change your identity by changing your mind. The word "repent" comes from the French word *penser*, to think. To repent means to think again. We tend to associate "repent" with a particular kind of mind change, one that has to do with stopping sinning. Well, when you think negative things about yourself, you create a loser's identity — and that is a form of sinning. Creating a loser's identity is limiting and a signal that it's time to rethink, change your mind, and create a positive self-image. Remember, you're the boss, and attitude is a matter of choice.

In Chapter 3, I discussed power statements. Power statements are identity statements. You can use them to define and strengthen your identity. As I said before, your power statement should represent who you are and what you aspire to be. It should be a mix of truths and affirmations.

Exercise 4 ➡

Prepare your own personal identity statement. Write down a statement of who you are (or could be) at your best. Affirm all of your strengths and highlight your potential. If you haven't yet manifested a desired quality, incorporate it into your identity statement. Read this statement to yourself. Repeat it often. Let it become you.

Psychologists who do ability testing know that the absence of a high score doesn't necessarily mean a lack of ability. It simply means that the person being tested didn't perform well on that day. When you have a poor shift or a poor game, don't lock onto that disappointing perception and keep rerunning it as an identity program of who you are. Instead, use it; say to yourself, "That's not who I am." Then imagine skating with speed and power, performing well, and enjoying the game. Remember, to increase your performance identity, and your confidence, think and see yourself at your best, then work toward making it a reality.

For too many athletes, their sense of well-being is determined by how they perform. If they do well, they feel good about themselves. If they perform poorly, they feel terrible or worthless. It's normal for people who are highly motivated — and who work very hard to achieve certain performance goals — to be disappointed with a poor performance. However, it's important to stay positively focused on your commitment. Remember and affirm that you are on a positive track, and that nothing can take you off that track. If you have a good practice or game, acknowledge yourself. Rerun your highlight reel — either on video or with mental-rehearsal imagery. Repeat your affirmations and power thoughts. On the other hand, if you have a poor shift, practice, or game, don't let that result shake your confidence. Instead, say, "That's not who I am," and then see yourself making the play(s).

I asked Pavel Bure what he says to himself during the game to keep himself positively focused. His answer contained some good advice, especially for those who tend to overreact to their performance on each and every shift. He said, "The two things I say to myself are 'Don't get frustrated' and 'Just keep working hard.'"

Pride

Most players have heard the word and most coaches have used it. I asked a 14-year-old bantam player what pride meant to her. Without a moment's hesitation she replied, "It's feeling good about what I do — and what my team does."

Pride is a composite of many aspects of a winning attitude. It's related to motivation, commitment, confidence, identity, and self-esteem. Pride means having a positive sense of who you are, how you choose to represent yourself, and what you have done. In hockey, pride is related to self as well as to team. If your identity is that of somebody who is motivated and committed to being the best he can be, it follows that you take pride in performing well. To play well requires preparation, so you would also take pride in preparing to be at your best.

Pride in your team means that you identify with (or tie your self-image to) the team's performance; you commit, and you derive satisfaction from the team playing well. When a team is successful, the confidence and pride of its players increases. However, pride isn't exactly the same as winning. It's about doing your best. That often means success.

How do you grow pride? I turned to an expert, Mark Messier, who for more than 20 years has been the embodiment of pride and a winning attitude. I asked Mark how he would coach a young player to develop pride. He responded that there is no simple answer. So many things go into developing a sense of pride, he said, including the way a child is brought up, his values, his work ethic, and his self-esteem. And people are different. What inspires some people is completely different from what motivates and drives others. Some people feel proud when they win. Others win and feel disappointed.

Mark went on to say that Canadians think of themselves as living in the best hockey nation in the world. They take pride in how they play the game. If a player is selected to put on a Team Canada jersey, there's a real sense of pride that goes with that. That sense of pride moves the player to want to play and be as good as he can be because of what it stands for — and because of who he is.

"If I had to pin it down," Mark concluded, "I guess pride is about being your best. It's meeting your expectations and those of others. But most importantly, it's meeting the expectations you set for yourself."

Exercise 5 ➡

Follow these eight steps for building pride.

1. Relax and breathe. Begin to think about and imagine yourself playing to the best of your ability, really playing well. Visualize the good stuff.
2. Run through your ABCs. See yourself making all the plays. Acknowledge that image. Say, "That's who I am." Take on that identity of yourself at your best.
3. Make the commitment to be the best you can be.
4. Do the work to make it happen — in the weight room, on the bike, on the ice, at practice. Combine all that with mental training.
5. Be consistent. Work at it every day. Give 100 percent every game. Every shift.
6. Evaluate your progress. Find something positive to acknowledge, even if it's only your dedication and work ethic. Find some area that needs more attention and improvement.
7. Walk your talk. Model your commitment and determination to your teammates.
8. As you do, as you put your heart and soul into it, slowly and surely your sense of pride in who you are, what you are trying to accomplish, and what you are able to do, will grow every day.

Love of the Game

In the last three chapters I've talked about "power programs" — the thoughts, images, and attitudes that you can use to generate the energy, emotion, and direction that help you perform at your best. Remember, thoughts and images are energy. You have a personal connection to an unlimited source of energy in the form of power words and high-performance images that you can use to enhance your game. Remember, attitude is a matter of choice and you're the boss.

I want to add a power word to the list of suggestions that you received earlier. I encourage you to use the word and see whether — and how — it can be useful for you. The power word I want you to add is *love*. Love is an antidote to fear, which is the greatest limiting program that people run on their mental TVs.

Fear has many faces. It can be fear of failure, fear of embarrassment, fear of falling short of expectations, fear of letting the team down, fear of getting hurt, fear of losing control, fear of the unknown, and even fear of success. As I've said several times, fear causes tension and contraction. Fear cuts down breathing. Fear reduces energy flow and fear limits performance.

Love is more powerful than fear. Love is expansive. It opens us up to new possibilities. While fear can motivate a good performance, love can inspire great performances. As human beings, love is one of the greatest forces available to us. When we combine love with talent and training, remarkable things are possible.

Interesting? Perhaps. But does it relate to hockey? Absolutely. Love is at the core of winning hockey. When he anounced his retirement, Wayne Gretzky was asked what advice he had for young players starting off in the game today. Gretzky's advice was not to play hockey for whatever you might get out of it in the end — such as money or fame — but to play hockey because you love it. And play as if you love it. Good things may flow from that. That sentiment is echoed by many of the players I have worked with. Over and over again they tell me that when they play with passion, they feel like kids enjoying the game — and they play their best hockey.

Grow your passion for the game. Choose something to love in every hockey situation. Use the pressures and the challenges. Before a big game against an intimidating opponent, think, "I love the game. I love to compete. I love the challenge. I love to be pushed to be my best."

Love produces ease. Fear produces dis-ease. To make the most of any situation, even a challenging one, choose it, use it, love it, and transform it.

Exercise 6 ➡

Recall some of the hockey imagery that we discussed earlier. Imagine feeling strong on your skates, moving well, making good reads, being aggressive, and being smooth with the puck. Imagine going into the corner against a bigger, stronger player. Imagine getting good position, being low and balanced. Imagine winning the puck. Again, love the challenge. Love beating the big men. Love dominating the smaller guys. Love being out there on the edge. Love pushing the envelope. Love making a good pass. Love to score.

Thinking "love thoughts" can change your feelings and make it easier to handle any challenging situations. Love produces ease. Fear produces dis-ease. It's your choice. You're the boss.

Your passion for the game can help you to tap a limitless power source. Fear stimulates action; it can kick-start you to get going. Imagine a bear chasing you through the woods. You are racing ahead of it. You're frightened. You're tense. You are trying to go fast. You would probably move very quickly. But the greatest performances come when people go beyond fear and move into the love zone. Again, love to skate, love to check, love to hit, love to score, love to dominate, love the challenge, love being there, love to compete, love quality competition, love pushing yourself into the unknown. Love the game.

The game of hockey is like a mirror. It's an opportunity to learn and to grow — to discover what you have to work on to become a better athlete and to empower yourself. Many people use fear of failure to push themselves to succeed, and they run themselves down when they don't perform well. Go beyond making failure a negative driver. It's tough to live like that. Instead, think "I love the challenge. I'm committed to using it. I don't need to achieve something in order to be something. I'm okay and I'm getting better." Start by being positive about yourself, and find something to love in every hockey situation.

Hockey is a game of passion. Find things to love about how you play the game.

HOMEWORK ⇢

There are four homework assignments for Chapter 5.

Assignment 1 ⇢

Explore your commitment. Set some goals. Set goals for the month, for the week, for the next game, and for the next practice. See yourself working toward your goals and overcoming any possible obstacles. One of the keys to commitment is learning how to use adversity to make you stronger.

Assignment 2 ⇢

Take a look at your identity and confidence. Think of your strengths as a player and fill in the blanks.

Write down "I am a good _____."

Consider the elements that make you effective. Note what you have to do to maintain these strengths. Develop a training program (with steps and stages) to maintain your competence at the things you are good at. As you work on your program, use your positive self-talk, power words, and imagery. Strengthen your identity as someone who is good at _____.

Think of an area in which you must improve as a player. Write down "I am improving my _____."

Consider the elements necessary for you to be competent in this area. List what you would have to do to improve. Develop a training schedule (with steps and stages) to improve in this area. As you work on your program, use your positive self-talk, power words, and imagery. Grow your identity as someone who is good at _____

_____ .

Assignment 3 ⟶

Review and edit your identity statement (see Exercise 4). Repeat it to yourself at least once a day, and twice on game days. Make it a regular part of your training program and preparation.

Assignment 4 ⟶

Grow your passion for the game. Choose things to love about the game of hockey and your situation. Start to use "love" as a power word in your training. Love is one of the most powerful forces you can have working for you. Love to play. Love to train. Love to compete. Love a challenge. Love to check. Love to score. Love to compete with the big guys. Love to dominate the small guys. Love yourself. Love the situation you're in.

Continue working with all your power words. Keep using them. Repetition builds strength. If a couple of words don't feel right to you, let them go. Always be on the lookout for new words. Add a new word, drop a word that you're not using or that doesn't seem to have power for you.

Chapter 6

What Does It Take to Make It?

I asked several NHL scouts and coaches the following question: "What does it take to make it in the NHL? Specifically, what are the psychological qualities that you look for in young talent?" Here's what they had to say.

Jim Nill was a tough-checking winger for several teams, including the Vancouver Canucks and Detroit Red Wings. Now the assistant general manager of the Wings, Jim has been scouting young talent for many years. He says teams look for "character." They look for young players with a passion for the game — players who won't give up, no matter what obstacles get in their way. People like Chris Chelios, Tiger Williams, and Dave Taylor were all young players of questionable talent who went on to become NHL stars because of their determination, work ethic, and competitiveness.

Ron Delorme, another former NHL checker and now a senior

scout for the Vancouver Canucks, says, "Of course we look for skating ability and size. But I also look at a player's character and his willingness to compete." When I asked Ron what he meant by character, he said, "Grit, determination, and mental toughness. It's not just about being the biggest and strongest. It's the desire to get in there and give it what you've got. That's what I look for."

Bart Bradley, a senior scout with the Boston Bruins, introduced me to "the five S's" that he said some scouts use to evaluate young players. They are: skating, size, skill, sense, and spirit. He said spirit is as important as any of the others. When I asked him what he meant by spirit, he said, "Plain and simple, it's about a player's guts — his willingness to go into the corners and fight for the puck."

Mike Penny, the director of player personnel for the Toronto Maple Leafs, has been evaluating young hockey talent for 30 years. Mike says what he looks for is quite simple: "Can he play or can't he play? His ability to play at an NHL level comes down to three things: his ability to skate; having a good feel for the game; and not being afraid." If a player has all three of these tools, Mike says, it's a pretty sure bet he can play in the NHL. He might even make it with two of the three.

As we spoke about different players, some of whom had been successful and those who had failed to make it, Mike added two other factors to the definition of "character": work ethic and passion for the game. "Skills can be developed," Mike says, "but if a player is afraid, that doesn't change. Work ethic is something that a person grows up with, and it's also difficult to change. The young men who make it in this league are tough, reliable players who have a good work ethic and love to play. The players who won't make it in the game are the lazy guys. Few of them ever change and they are a constant struggle for their coaches."

Frank Jay, the senior scout for the Ottawa Senators, is another individual who has been prospecting talent for decades. Frank said he looks for skating, speed, size, instincts, and toughness. Beyond those qualities, he said, he looks for character. When I asked him what character meant to him, Frank replied, "I want to know if the kid is sincere and if he's a good person. It's not always easy to tell, but it's very important."

"Are you saying that if you saw a player with good physical attributes, someone who was a good, tough player but who wasn't a good person, that you wouldn't be interested in him?"

"Yes," Frank said. "That's what I'm saying. I think it's important for us to select good people."

Harry Neale, the longtime analyst with *Hockey Night in Canada*, is a former NHL head coach and general manager. He pointed to two qualities he thought were shared by successful players: talent and a passion for the game. "The degree to which a player loves the game determines whether or not he'll be a great player," Harry said.

"A big part of Gordie Howe's greatness was his love of the game and his dedication to it," Harry added. "It was a passion that Howe kept alive throughout his career. When a player starts to think, 'What am I going to do when I stop playing hockey?' there's a shift in mindset and a decrease in passion that does more to end his career then old and tired legs."

Head and Heart

In Chapter 1 I talked about integrating head and heart. Being a complete player is about playing with both your head and your heart. Shayne Corson, a tough NHL forward and team leader, says, "It doesn't matter if you have talent if you won't the pay the price and play the system."[1]

I watched a junior game with John Chapman, the Philadelphia Flyers head scout. He was looking at a talented young winger with good skill and obvious scoring ability. "These things are important qualities," he said. "So are size and skating ability. But we also look at a player's makeup. Specifically, we want to know how he deals with pressure situations. We also try to assess a player's determination, his work ethic, and his passion for the game." A term John used to describe a player's toughness and willingness to go into the

---

1 Interview broadcast on CKNW Radio (Vancouver), April 9, 2000.

corners was "battle level." That night, the young winger's battle level could have been more impressive.

Testing

One of the things that makes a scout's job challenging is reading a young player's potential and predicting who will grow into an NHL player. Character is a significant factor in making that determination, and it is not something that can be easily measured. Chapman mentioned that his team, like a few of the others in the league, use psychological tests in an attempt to improve their assessment of prospective NHL players.

These tests are standardized interviews in which a player's responses are compared with the response patterns of other athletes who have succeeded — and failed — in the past.

One psychological test I have used with athletes in a variety of sports is the Athletic Success Profile (ASP). It's also used by several NHL teams. The test looks at 11 different factors, including drive, determination, leadership, emotional control, coachability, trust, aggressiveness, responsibility, self-confidence, mental toughness, and conscientiousness. What follows are the ASP's definitions of each of the 11 traits.

Drive

The player has the desire or need to win, to achieve, and to be successful in athletics; desires to attain athletic excellence; responds positively to competitive situations; aspires to accomplish difficult tasks; sets and maintains high goals in athletics.

Determination

The player shows the willingness to put forth the physical effort necessary to be successful; is persistent and unrelenting in his work habits; practices long and hard; works on skills until exhausted; works independently; does not give up easily on a problem.

Leadership

The player has the desire to influence or direct others in athletics; assumes the role of leader naturally and spontaneously; enjoys the responsibility and challenge of being a leader; attempts to control the environment and to influence or direct others; makes decisions and expresses opinions in a forceful manner.

Emotional control

The player is capable of maintaining composure during the stress of athletic competition; can face stress in a calm, objective manner; rarely allows feelings to affect performance; is not easily discouraged, depressed, or frustrated by bad breaks, calls, or mistakes.

Coachability

The player shows respect for coaches and the coaching process; considers receiving coaching essential to becoming a good athlete; is receptive to coaches' advice; cooperates with athletic authorities; accepts the leadership of the team captain.

Trust

The player accepts and believes in people; believes what coaches and fellow athletes say; is free of jealous tendencies; tends to get along well with fellow athletes.

Aggressiveness

The player believes that taking the offensive is crucial to winning; tends to initiate action and take the offensive; releases aggression readily; is ready and willing to use force to get the job done; will not allow others to be pushy; may try to "get even" with people.

Responsibility

The player accepts responsibility for the consequences of his actions, including mistakes; accepts blame and criticism, even when not deserved; can endure physical and mental pain; may dwell on mistakes and impose self-punishment.

Self-confidence

The player believes that he has the ability needed to be successful in sports; has an unfaltering trust in self and feels sure of personal powers, abilities, and skills; handles unexpected situations well; makes decisions with assurance; may be quick to express beliefs, ideas, and opinions to coaches and other athletes.

Mental toughness

The player is able to accept strong criticism and setbacks without competing less effectively; does not become easily upset when losing or competing poorly; does not need excessive praise or encouragement from coach; recovers quickly when things go wrong.

Conscientiousness

The player displays willingness to do things according to the rules; will not attempt to bend the rules to suit personal needs; may tend to be exacting in character and dominated by a sense of duty; places the good of the group ahead of personal well-being; does not try to con the coach or other players.

If you are a player, you might find it useful to assess yourself in regard to each of these traits and adjust accordingly. If you would like more input, ask your coach or a teammate to meet with you and discuss his perception of you in regard to these qualities. Awareness put to use equals power. Become more aware of your strengths, but also those areas in which you could improve to become more effective.[2]

Exercise 1 ⇒

Assess yourself in each of the 11 attributes listed below. Evaluate yourself on a scale of 1 to 5, with 1 being extremely low and 5

2 If you are a player who wants a professional personal evaluation, or if you are a coach and want a team evaluation of these traits, contact AthleticSuccess.com.

being extremely high. Put a checkmark in the space that best describes you.

Attribute	1	2	3	4	5
Drive	_____	_____	_____	_____	_____
Determination	_____	_____	_____	_____	_____
Leadership	_____	_____	_____	_____	_____
Emotional control	_____	_____	_____	_____	_____
Coachability	_____	_____	_____	_____	_____
Trust	_____	_____	_____	_____	_____
Aggressiveness	_____	_____	_____	_____	_____
Responsibility	_____	_____	_____	_____	_____
Self-confidence	_____	_____	_____	_____	_____
Mental toughness	_____	_____	_____	_____	_____
Conscientiousness	_____	_____	_____	_____	_____

If you want additional input, ask your coach to do the same, then compare and discuss your findings.

Exercise 2 ➡

Having defined one or two areas in which you could improve your winning hockey attitude in Exercise 1, create a training plan to develop your strength in these areas. For example, if you evaluated yourself as low on emotional control, you might work with the exercises in Chapter 2. If determination is an area that you want to improve, work on goal-setting. Set a goal for the season, for each month and week, and for each practice. Write your goal(s) down and repeat them to yourself often. Then see that you do the work necessary to achieve the goals you've set.

⚬

A pro team asked me to assess their captain. The evaluation consisted of spending some time with him in an informal interview, and then, with his permission, doing some testing. One of the tests I used was the ASP. What we found on that test was very interesting.

On most scales, the captain's scores were average to respectably high. But there were some unusual findings. On the self-confidence scale, his score was in the top (99th) percentile. But his aggressiveness score was very low (11th percentile) and his determination score was also low (38th percentile).

I wasn't sure exactly what this meant until I discussed the findings with the player and his coaches. Then it became clearer. The player was a "gamer." He was an outstanding athlete and extremely confident in his abilities to perform in any situation. Under pressure, in a big game or in the playoffs, he would play great. However, his behavior in practice was disappointing. In part because of his considerable confidence in his athletic ability, he didn't expend effort or exert himself in practice the way he could or should. Nor did he push his teammates to work hard in practice. As a consequence, the team underachieved.

It was explained to the captain that, as a leader, a star, and a role model for his teammates, he set the work standard for the group. And that few if any of his teammates had either his remarkable athletic skills or his underlying confidence. They needed to work very hard in practice to play more effectively and confidently in games. He would have to model that work ethic and push his teammates to be better prepared. When he understood that his lack of effort in practice had a less than positive impact on others, his behavior in practice improved and eventually, so did the team's performance.

Mental Toughness

The elements of character that professional scouts point to most frequently are commitment, determination, passion for the game, and mental toughness. These are the mental software programs they are searching for in future NHL stars. We discussed commitment and passion in Chapter 5. Now I want to talk about mental toughness.

In an aggressive, physical, high-speed, collision sport like hockey, it's not surprising that you can often hear players, coaches, and scouts talk about mental toughness. There are many definitions of what mental toughness means, from "guts" to good concentration. The ASP definition of mental toughness is "the ability to accept strong criticism and setbacks without competing less effectively." According to the ASP, the player with mental toughness does not become easily upset when losing or competing poorly, does not need excessive praise or encouragement from the coach, and recovers quickly when things go wrong.

I see mental toughness as the ability to focus on the challenge or task at hand without being distracted by peripheral events. In a game, mental toughness might express itself as an unwillingness to ease up when your team is down by two goals — or ahead by two. It causes you to play every shift as if it will decide the outcome of the game.

If you're mentally tough, you don't let yourself get distracted. Imagine you're playing in a close game, down by a goal, and your team has the man advantage. Somebody deals you a cheap shot. Instead of retaliating (and possibly costing your team a power-play opportunity), you stay focused on working to generate a scoring chance for your team.

Billy Smith, the former goalie for the New York Islanders, was a mentally tough competitor. He says, "I never retaliated. I always initiated. There's a big difference." Reminiscing about the 1981–82 Stanley Cup finals, Billy said, "We [the Islanders] had an understanding not to retaliate and not to fight. And we didn't. Even when Tiger Williams ripped the chain right off my neck, I wouldn't fight. The Canucks did. They took the penalties and we scored."

Duane Sutter, another member of those Islander championship teams, agrees with Smith's dictum to initiate and not to retaliate. "Al Arbour [former coach of the Islanders] used to say, 'If you're ready to play, you initiate. If you're not ready, you end up playing from behind all night long.'"

During the 2000–2001 season, Adam Deadmarsh provided an excellent example of mental toughness. Two things happened during the season that highlighted Deadmarsh's resolve. The first incident occurred while he was playing for the Colorado Avalanche.

In a game with Vancouver Canucks, Deadmarsh's aggressive play around the net led to a fight with Ed Jovanovski. In the course of the fight, Deadmarsh was knocked out cold. The resulting concussion kept him off the ice for several weeks. In his first game back against Vancouver following the concussion I was curious to see if Deadmarsh's play around the net would be any less aggressive and if he would be intimidated around the defender who had knocked him out a month earlier. True to his character, Deadmarsh played his usual aggressive, go-for-it brand of hockey. Late in the game with his team in the lead he challenged the defenseman to a rematch. The bout ended in a draw but his willingness to engage signalled Deadmarsh's unwillingness to allow the beating he suffered change his style of play or his identity in any way.

A second and more significant example of his mental toughness occurred later in the season. A blockbuster trade sent Deadmarsh and teammate Aaron Miller to the Los Angeles Kings for the Kings' captain, Rob Blake. For Deadmarsh it was a shocking move — from a team that had the best record in the NHL and a Cup favorite to a team that was well out of the playoff picture at the time of the trade. It is difficult for any player to move from number one to number 20, especially a core player like Deadmarsh, who was closely connected with his Avalanche teammates. What made the move especially upsetting was that just a couple of days before the trade Deadmarsh's wife had given birth to twins who were seriously ill.

Once again Deadmarsh demonstrated his mental toughness. He refocused on the new task at hand and became one of the key factors in a remarkable Kings' turnaround that led them into the playoffs and past the favored Detroit Red Wings in the first round — and to game seven against the Avalanche in the next round.

Reflecting on the experience Deadmarsh said simply, " It took me two days to get over it when I was traded, but then we buckled down and made the playoffs." The complete player uses everything. This player certainly demonstrated the mental toughness to do just that.

Mental toughness is expressed in your consistent determination to do what's necessary and your focus to get it done no matter what. If you're a scorer and you haven't scored in several games, if you're a checker or a defenseman and your check gets open in front of the net and scores, if for whatever reason you've been benched or are getting little ice time, mental toughness is that quality that won't let you get down on yourself, your teammates, or the coach, but instead encourages you to stay positive and work hard to express your ability and reach your goal.

A junior team I was working with had just clinched its league championship by winning a close, hard-fought game. During the game, I was sitting and talking with a player who had been a healthy scratch. This young defenseman's repeated complaints that he wasn't getting enough ice time or the chance to rush the puck as freely as he did the year before, when he was at the midget level, disturbed me. There was little apparent interest or joy at his team's success in a tough game. While I could understand his personal frustration and disappointment about not playing more, focusing on his distress and broadcasting it at that time was more "me" than "we," and it reflected a lack of mental toughness.

Jack McIlhargey, a veteran NHL defenseman who is now an assistant coach with the Vancouver Canucks, says, "Mental toughness means not letting things get to you. If you make a mistake on the ice, you don't dwell on it. Don't carry it with you. Instead, you get yourself ready for the next shift. Mental toughness is that ability to stay focused on the positive."

Here's a way in which mental toughness might express itself in practice. Imagine you're tired. You've played a number of games recently and you feel it. Practice is over, but there's ice time available and you are determined to improve your skating. So, instead of hanging with the guys, you stay on the ice and do extra power-skating exercises to improve your conditioning or to develop into the player you want to become. It takes mental toughness to work on the things that you are not good at and don't especially enjoy.

Mental toughness is expressed through discipline and hard work over the summer months — doing more than the minimum amount of training and arriving in camp in excellent shape.

After an injury, mental toughness is what gives you that ability to focus on climbing back up the mountain instead of surrendering to the frustration and disappointment that arise out of lost opportunity, lost conditioning, and enduring the pain and sweat necessary to get you back where you want to be. It's what enables you to follow your rehabilitation program and move forward one step at a time.

Mattias Ohlund reported to training camp for his third NHL season in exceptional shape. He had worked very hard all summer on his conditioning and had an exceptional camp. Then, in the team's fifth preseason game, he was struck directly in the eye by a puck from a slap shot traveling at more than 90 miles per hour. It was a serious injury. There was considerable internal bleeding in the eye and there was concern that Mattias might lose his sight in that eye. He was ordered to rest completely for a month to minimize the possibility of further hemorrhaging. It was very difficult for a motivated player who had just spent 12 weeks training intensively to get into the best shape in his life to simply "do nothing." But it had to be done. And it was done, without complaint.

Then the slow road back began. It included rest, surgery on the eye, more rest, and medication. Then, after two months, little steps like going for a walk, supervised light training in the gym, and more intensive training. Then, there was on-ice training — light at first, with no contact, then some contact drills, then finally, full contact.

Four months after the injury, Mattias was back in the lineup — not in the ideal shape he had been in at the start of the season, but still expected to handle the speed and pressure of playing defense in the NHL. In his first game back he played more than 20 minutes. Two games later, his workload jumped to 30 minutes. He struggled with his conditioning at first, and was criticized in the press, but never once through that entire process did I ever hear Mattias complain or offer an excuse. By the end of the year he was playing excellent hockey. That's mental toughness.

Mental toughness is mind over matter. Chris Pronger describes it as "having that feeling that your legs are just too tired, but still working hard and toughing it out."

Being sent to the minors can challenge one's mental toughness. Trent Klatt had scored over 20 goals in a season for the Philadelphia Flyers. Then, after a disappointing season and a half with the Vancouver Canucks, he was sent down to the AHL. The demotion was difficult for an established, respected NHLer to take. It was made even more difficult by the fact that Trent's family had to be uprooted and relocated once again. Many pros would have become negative, but Trent didn't. He took the assignment as an opportunity and used it.

Trent worked very hard in the American league. He regained his scoring touch, overcame a painful foot injury, and, because of his excellent play, earned himself another opportunity with the Canucks. When he returned to the Vancouver lineup, he played extremely well. For the rest of the season, and into the next, he was one of the team's hardest-working players in every game and on every shift. Nothing seemed to distract him.

I saw Trent's ability to use the situation rather than letting it use him as an example of mental toughness, of a player using his mind to turn things around. He says, "I love to play hockey, both offense and defense. But when I [first arrived in Vancouver] I began worrying about defense, just defense. I let things distract me, and the game stopped being fun. When I was sent down to Syracuse, I was determined to use the opportunity to refocus and play like I knew I could play. That meant to becoming more aggressive on offense, making things happen, staying positive, and having fun. So I did."

Mental toughness is expressed in getting "up" to compete hard every day throughout the long hockey season. When I asked Scott Gomez how he was adjusting to his rookie year in the NHL, he said, "One of the things that's important is to stay focused. There's so much happening, so much positive and negative energy. You have to know how to handle it. Whether you've had a good game or a bad game, you have to be able to psych yourself — especially at this top level. I try not to get too high or too low. Sure, I celebrate a little when I score, but then it's back to focusing on what you've got to do on your next shift or in your next game. What's helped me so far is going back to my breathing and thinking positive — and about my ABCs."

Mental toughness is about all of the above. It manifests itself in disciplined, focused, positive, goal-directed behavior. Some people say it's not a teachable quality — either you are born mentally tough or you are not. I don't agree. Early experience and upbringing are undoubtedly big factors in developing mental toughness, but it is about focus, and focus is something you can control.

＝◯

You can make yourself mentally tougher by working on the following six skill areas.

Goal-setting. Know that you are response-able and know what you want. Have a clear sense of direction and purpose. Define your goal(s). It's much easier to stay focused and on course if you have a course to stay on.

Mastering your emotions. Learn how to change channels and stay centered. That means release, breathe, and refocus on what you want to make happen, in any situation.

Creating positive imagery. Generate positive pictures of where you are going and what you want to do on the ice. Create success images that support your motivation and drive. Do mental rehearsal to increase your focus and competence. Be a tiger, panther, or bear. Build a powerful, positive self-image that will help you play winning hockey and realize your goal.

Engaging in positive self-talk. Say positive things to yourself. Acknowledge your effort and your successes. Use your challenges and difficulties.

Being willing to work hard and being in great shape. Fatigue makes us vulnerable to doubt. Being in great shape builds confidence and supports positive focus and determination, all of which are the building blocks of mental toughness.

Dave "Tiger" Williams, who in his playing days was known as one of the NHL's toughest, says, "When you get fitness-tested, work to be in the top percentile of your team. It will help you keep going and give you a greater chance to succeed." Dave played for Toronto, Vancouver, Detroit, Los Angeles, and Hartford, and he adds, "If you are traded from a good team to a bad team, it can be very difficult to get up and stay positive when your chances of winning each night seem remote. But mental toughness is about playing hard every night, on every shift, on every team. And conditioning and commitment make that more possible."

Growing a winning attitude. Be a pro. Be committed to using everything. Whatever comes up, use it, learn from it, dominate it. Grow your confidence with preparation. Grow your identity as someone who is determined. And grow your passion for the game.

"Park it." Some sport psychologists have used the concept of "parking" to describe the experience of tuning out irrelevant thoughts and staying tuned in to what's appropriate. If a thought comes to mind that isn't going to help you perform or that you think may interfere with your on-ice performance, change the channel and park it.

For example, if an opposing player taunts you, slashes you, or tries to provoke or distract you in a close game, instead of reacting or retaliating and hurting your team, park that thought — and file it for later. If it's not something you can forget, then even the score some other time when it won't hurt your team. If you are having distracting or disturbing thoughts relating to off-ice issues and it's time to prepare for the game, park those thoughts for now and deal with them later.

Parking requires both perspective and emotional control, and these are qualities of mental toughness. Your ability to stop a thought, change channels, and park it is a combination of your motivation and your ability to release, breathe, and refocus.

Ask Paul Kariya how he deals with the high sticks, late hits, clutching and grabbing, and other frustrations in the game today, he'll tell you: "Getting angry doesn't accomplish anything. It doesn't help me to score."

Paul was introduced to the concept of parking it when he was in the Canadian national junior program. And it's something he still uses today. "I'm an offensive player. My job is to play offense. It's not to retaliate. If someone chops or slashes me, I park it and refocus. The ultimate way to get even is to put the puck in their net."

When I discuss mental discipline with young hockey players, there's something I'm fond of telling them: "When I walk through my neighborhood and my neighbor's dog barks, I don't bark back." I have said this dozens of times. Usually when I do, most players smile and nod. They can appreciate that it's ridiculous to bark back at a barking dog. However, on the ice, when someone on the other team barks at them, many players lose perspective and focus and they bark back.

My advice is not to go there. Ignore it. If you do notice the provocation, use it — or it will use you. How can you use it? As always, take a breath, release (anger, tension, frustration, fear, or whatever), and focus instead on the positive — on what you want to do on the ice, on your ABCs. Mental toughness is about maintaining that positive focus, no matter what.

As Tiger Williams says, "It used to be that if you got scored on, you might smash your stick on the ice and break it to show people that you were really pissed off and that you cared. Now if you do that, they think you're an idiot, and that all you care about is your own feelings."

Mike Johnston, an assistant coach with the Vancouver Canucks, says: "People who are mentally tough are resilient. They always believe they are going to find a way to do it, and they keep working to make it happen." These people draw heavily on positive past experiences. They've done it before and they know they can, and will, do it again. Explained this way, you can see that mental toughness is closely related to confidence — and like confidence it flows from success. Mike went on to say, "That's why teams like to have successful veterans, 'winners,' on the team. Their confidence and mental toughness have a positive impact on others."

When I asked Mike about mental-toughness training, he related a story that a basketball coach had passed on to him years before. Jack Donahue had asked his young daughter to look in the mirror and tell him who she saw. At first the girl said, "Me," and then she began to describe her physical attributes.

"What I see," said her father, "is a beautiful girl who can do anything." Thereafter, whenever he asked his daughter the question, her response was, "I see a beautiful girl who can do anything."

It's a nice story, an example of good parental coaching and a small piece in the puzzle to growing confidence and self-esteem.

One way to grow confidence is to be positive, to focus on possibility, and to say positive, empowering things to yourself. However, to really become mentally tough, you have to "go for it." You have to enter the war zone, that crucible of human experience, to really temper the steel of character. By that I mean you have to face challenges and succeed. You have to compete and win. You have to experience adversity and prevail. In becoming a more complete player, there are no substitutes for experience. Only through personal experience, through sweat, effort, trials, and tears do we learn that we can — and that we will, if we persevere and continue to do our best.

Chapter 7

Personality Differences on Ice

Players differ in terms of such physical attributes as size, strength, and speed. They also differ psychologically in terms of their attitude, experience, intelligence, and personality. In this chapter we will take a look at how these differences may affect the way to prepare for and play the game, and how to deal with pressure.

In addition to the Athletic Success Profile discussed in Chapter 6, a test that I frequently use to measure personality differences is the Myers-Briggs Type Indicator (MBTI). This test looks at four separate aspects of personality style. The three most relevant to our discussion of winning hockey are called extroversion-introversion, sensing-intuition, and feeling-thinking.

Extroversion versus Introversion

You may recall that in Chapter 2 I said there is a direct relationship between the amount of emotion or arousal a person experiences and his or her performance. With either too much or too little arousal, performance is less than optimal. The relationship is depicted in the following graph.

The relationship between arousal and performance can be complicated by a personality style factor like introversion/extroversion. In general, introverts tend to be more sensitive and may be more affected by pressure. They overload more easily than extroverts. In contrast, extroverts tend to be more stimulus-seeking and may require a higher level of

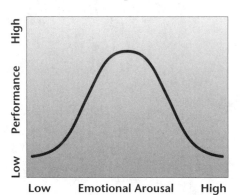

arousal to be at their best. This relationship is depicted as follows.

What this can mean in terms of pregame preparation is that, since introverts "over-arouse" more readily than extroverts, they may play better if they learn ways to stay calm before a game. Introverts seem to function best within a clearly defined pregame routine. This reduces unnecessary last-minute surprises and limits "rushing," both of which can be arousing and anxiety-{producing.

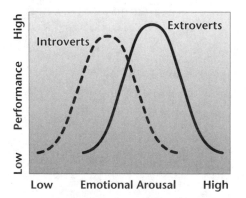

Introverts prefer things to be on time and take pride in having their equipment in order. This is a useful behavior. A possible downside, however, is that introverts sometimes become preoccupied with the minor details and rituals of preparation and small deviations in their pregame pattern can upset them. To allay any potential anxiety, it can be useful to remind the more introverted player (or coach) to relax. They can benefit by being reassured that they are prepared, that everything will be fine, and that they can deal with any minor alteration (in routine or schedule) that may present itself. A pregame breathing session, positive self-talk, and mental rehearsal are all useful mental skills for an introverted player.

Extroverts may actually require stimulation, interaction, and challenges to get into their optimal arousal zone. They may find it hard to organize well in advance, often needing last-minute urgency to get them going. This can lead to some confusion regarding equipment and scheduling. It's advisable to encourage extroverts to develop a pregame preparation routine that helps them do what they need to do to get themselves ready to play.

I remember Zeke, an extroverted team leader, talking trash on the bus on the way to a junior game. He expressed some of his anxiety by making critical comments about the team's effort in its last game and the previous day's practice, about the pregame schedule, the timing of their arrival at the rink, even the route the bus driver was taking to the game. When the team got into the dressing room and began to dress for the game, Zeke, who had been "so busy with so much," realized that he had forgotten to pack his skates.

It is important to be aware of who you are, who your teammates are, and to respect the differences that exist between people. You deserve to express your abilities — and so do they.

I have worked with many teams. Most have a wide range of personality styles. These differences can be reflected in musical preferences. Some players like to listen to loud rock before a game, some like heavy metal, others like calming music, and some prefer quiet. Music can be used to regulate emotional states. Understand what you like to do and listen to in order to feel ready to play. And become more aware of the needs of others. Respecting these differences and having some flexibility is an important part of successful team preparation. Not attending to individual differences is something that can cause a player or team problems, even at the highest levels of competition.

Another distinction between introverts and extroverts is that extroverts tend to be more social and outgoing. In getting up for the game, the extrovert is more apt to be energized by the competitive confrontation of "me [or us] against them." The introvert is more inwardly focused and may be more motivated by the personal challenge to perform well.

In regard to intra-team interaction, extroverts enjoy talking and joking with teammates before a game. Introverts, on the other hand, are more apt to prepare quietly. They often warm up and mentally rehearse aspects of their game by themselves. Joking around right before a game can be a disturbing distraction for them. I've also seen players (and coaches) who were aggressive extroverts use stimulation and confrontation to get themselves (and their teammates) "up" before and during the game. For some players a direct, in-your-face challenge can spark them to perform. For others, it has just the opposite effect.

In his first year in the NHL, one player (whom we can call Jones) was yelled at and sworn at by his coach so much that his teammates gave him the nickname "F'n." Every time the coach talked to — or about — Jones, he would say "F'n Jones did this," or "F'n Jones can't do that." A dozen years later, after Jones had established himself as a very competent NHL player, I asked him about the story. "Yeah, it's true," he confirmed. "And I want to tell you, it's no fun driving to work in the morning with your guts in a knot because you know the coach is going to yell and swear at you. It certainly didn't help me to play better. It was only later, when I was treated respectfully, that I become a better player."

Creating Your Own Preparation Regimen

A motivated and talented junior player I consulted with called and described what for him was a difficult situation. He said he was on a team where the coaches provided little discipline — "Lines change themselves" — little direction, and less than adequate feedback. He was concerned because he aspired to play professional hockey and he felt the lack of quality coaching was limiting his development. He had made an effort to talk to the coach, but reported that it hadn't made any difference. The trading deadline had passed and he was stuck where he was. He said he felt that he was losing respect for the program, and as a result his interest in playing the game was diminishing.

I understood his frustration. But if he wasn't getting the direction and feedback from his coaches, he would have to find a way to use the situation to become stronger. I suggested he create goals and a training structure for himself. I said, "For the rest of the season, set some reasonable, challenging performance goals, define some skills to work on in practice, work hard, and use your time effectively.

"You're 18 years old," I said. "You aren't a child any longer. If you're not getting what you need from others, work to create what you need for yourself."

In any situation, a player must take responsibility for knowing himself and what he needs to do to prepare and perform at his best.

I was talking to another team about preparation. "What's the best way to prepare?" one of the players asked. I said that preparation is a personal thing. There are many elements that go into quality preparation — rest, diet, practice, mental rehearsal, and power thinking are all important parts of preparing yourself to excel. "It's important for you to discover what you need to do to be most effective," I said.

The following preparation sheet provides a way of scheduling your time and energy, from before the game, right up to and through the game. Thinking things through in advance may help you get a clearer mental picture of exactly what to do to prepare and play well.

Exercise 1 ➡

Complete the following preparation sheet for an upcoming competition.

GAME DAY PREPARATION SHEET ⅢⅢ➡

Name: _____

Game: _____ Date: _____ Time: _____

Night before the Game:

Activity: _____ Bedtime: _____

Game Day Wake-up:

My alarm/wake-up call is set for: _____

My wake-up plan is (e.g., shower, walk, stretch):

_____

_____

Breakfast: Food: _____ Time: _____

Morning Activity:

Pregame skate: _____

Focus: _____

Treatment/Rehab? Yes_____ No_____

If yes, describe: _____

School (classes)/Work (to do) _____

Lunch: Food: _____ Time: _____

Afternoon Activity:

School (classes)/Work (to do) _____

Rest time: From _____ until _____

Relaxation/Breathing: _____

Imagery/Mental rehearsal: _____

Self-talk: _____

Dinner/Snacks: Food: _____ Time: _____

Things to do before I leave for the game (e.g., check equipment,

telephone): _____

Getting there (mode, route, with whom): _____

Departure time: _____ Arrival time at rink: _____

Pregame Activity:

Check equipment (skates/sticks/pads)

Physical treatment: _____

Mental preparation: _____

Relaxation/breathing: _____

Imagery/Mental rehearsal (ABCs):

_____

_____

_____

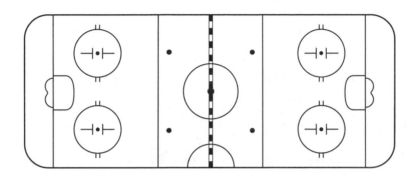

Self-talk (power words and thoughts for the game):

_____

_____

On-ice warmup: Focus: _____

In the dressing room: Focus: _____

During the Game (things to do/remember):

First shift: _____

ABCs: _____

Self-talk/Power words: _____

Between shifts, remember to _____

If there are long waits between shifts, remember to

_____

Between periods, remember to _____

At Any Time during the Game or between Periods:

If I'm feeling good: _____

If I'm feeling tight/anxious and want to reduce tension:

_____

If I'm negative: _____

If I'm hurt: _____

Under pressure and at crucial times, think:

_____

After the Game:

Evaluating my performance, I will continue to

_____

When I think of parts of my game that I have to strengthen, I will work to improve the following:

_____

Here is when and how I can work on this in practice and in games:

_____

Reflecting on my preparation for the game, I would adjust it
(if necessary) as follows:

_____

Here's an example of how a Junior A player filled out the inventory.

SAMPLE GAME DAY PREPARATION SHEET ⟶

Name: _# 18 John Smith_

Game: _Langley vs. Chilliwack_   Date: _Jan. 22_ Time: _7:00 p.m._

Night before the Game:

Activity: _Relax, watch TV_   Bedtime: _11:00 p.m._

Game Day Wake-up:

My alarm/wake-up call is set for: _7:00 p.m._

My wake-up plan is:

_____ _shower, walk, stretch_ _____

_____

Breakfast: Food: _cereal, toast, juice_   Time: _8:00 a.m._

Morning Activity:

Pregame skate: _not this morning_ _____

Focus: _____

Treatment/Rehab? Yes _____   No _X_____

If yes, describe: _____

School (classes)/Work (to do) _school classes_ _____

Lunch: Food: _juice, sandwich, granola bar_   Time: _12:30 p.m._

Afternoon Activity:

School (classes)/Work (to do) _school classes / Work (to do)_

Rest time: From _3:00 p.m._ until _4:00 p.m._

Relaxation/Breathing: _YES_

Imagery/Mental rehearsal: _Run ABCs_

Self-talk: _positive thoughts — I'm sharp! I'll play well!_

Dinner/Snacks: Food: _pasta, chicken, water_   Time: _4:15 p.m._

Things to do before I leave for the game: _check dress clothes_

Getting there (mode, route, with whom): _with John_

Departure time: _5:15 p.m._ Arrival time at rink: _5:30 p.m._

Pregame Activity:

Check equipment: _skates, sticks, pads_

Physical treatment: _no / tape wrist_

Mental preparation: _____

Relaxation/breathing: _____

Imagery/Mental rehearsal (ABCs):

replay + plays from last game!

Offense: A. Win the boards B. Good wheels / move my feet

C. Good passes Defense: A2. Come back hard B2. Angle my check

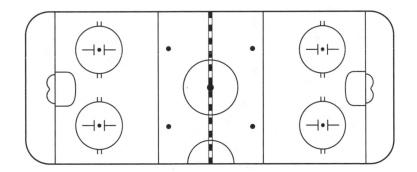

Self-talk (power words and thoughts for the game):

"Wheels, hands, eyes"

The boards are mine!

On-ice warmup: Focus: _Passes on the tape / shoot on net!_

In the dressing room: Focus: _____

During the Game (things to do/remember):

First shift: _Get in a hit, be physical, keep legs moving_

ABCs: _A. skate, skate B. passing C. shoot accurately_

Self-talk/Power words: _BE POSITIVE_

Between shifts, remember to _drink water, breathe, focus_

If there are long waits between shifts, remember to
STAY POSITIVE, FOCUS, ABCs

Between periods, remember to _hydrate, think – I can do better_

At Any Time during the Game or between Periods:

If I'm feeling good: _keep playing well, don't get too high_

If I'm feeling tight/anxious and want to reduce tension:
BREATHE, RELAX, THINK "SMOOTH"

If I'm negative: _change the channel, be positive, "that's who I am"_

If I'm hurt: _breathe — ice — trainer — focus next shift_

Under pressure and at crucial times, think:
think of ABCs, want the puck, tough "D," "I make things happen."

After the Game:

Evaluating my performance, I will continue to _work hard, stay_
focused, produce on offense, win the boards, make things happen

When I think of parts of my game that I have to strengthen, I will
work to improve the following:
on-the-tape pases, quick shots (accurate), finish my checks

Here is when and how I can work on this in practice and in games:
watch game video, work on shot before + after practice

Reflecting on my preparation for the game, I would adjust it
(if necessary) as follows:
I believe I have a good pregame routine and as long as I stick to
it, I will continue to be prepared and successful

Understanding who you are and what style works for you can be
very helpful. One thing you can do to gain insight is to recall those
days when you played your best. Think back and ask yourself,
"What did I do to prepare on those high-performance days?"

Exercise 2 ➡

Think back and visualize a game when you performed to the best of
your ability. Fill out the forms based on your activities that day.
Then do the same for a game in which you played poorly. Compare

the two. Note any significant differences that stand out. This may help you to identify and develop some pregame behaviors or a pregame routine that works for you.

John Vanbiesbrouck is a goalie with 17 years of NHL playing experience. I would describe John as thoughtful and serious about his pregame preparation. He has a definite game-day routine. He starts with a light breakfast. At the morning skate he focuses on preparing himself. Sometimes he watches the other team's shooters (but never their goalies). He avoids interviews the day of the game. He has his main pregame meal at 12:30 (usually a set menu high in carbohydrates, along with chicken or fish, but with no spices).

After the meal he relaxes and does some inspirational reading. Then he takes a nap. When he awakens, he watches TV (nothing too serious, and only for about half an hour). Then he has a light snack. He gets to the rink early so that he has time to do some visualization and stretching, then he dresses for the game.

During a game he always maintains his focus on the puck — even during stoppages in play. "My job is to stay focused on the puck and that's what I do for the entire game. I don't skate over to the bench during stoppages in play. I don't think it's the time to socialize."

One of the things that John and other, more technical goalies pride themselves on is their self-control, their ability to stay focused on the puck, and their ability not to be distracted by anything such as being bumped or screened or what happened in the last shift, the last period, or the last game. Goalies such as Billy Smith, Patrick Roy, and Garth Snow, who are more extroverted and enjoy getting involved in the action, stand at the other end of the spectrum. These goalies have been known to mix it up with opposing forwards who invade the crease or crash the net, and they come well out of the crease to play the puck in dangerous situations.

These extroverts who seem to thrive on confrontation have to remind themselves not to be *too* confrontational. A question to be evaluated by an extroverted goalie is whether being in the other player's face actually helps or hinders his play. If being bumped bothers him and causes him to retaliate, then he has fallen victim to a distraction that will throw him off his game. Extroverted goalies may find they must learn to manage their emotions and strengthen their focus.

Billy Smith has told me that if you play a more confrontational game, you have to be smart and have discipline. He also repeated a favorite line: "I never retaliated. I only initiated."

I often make audiotapes for players to use before games so that they can relax and visualize themselves playing well. These tapes usually consist of a brief, five-minute section on relaxing, breathing, and sending energy out through the body; then another five-minute section that combines right feelings with mentally rehearsing good offensive and defensive play. Not surprisingly, some players find the tapes more useful than others. I think the tapes are most effective when they are personalized to address a player's style, the specific behaviors he wants to rehearse, and the emotional state he wants to feel.

While I was working as a sport psychologist for the Los Angeles Kings, I made a generic pregame "warmup" tape for all the forwards. It contained the "right feeling, right focus" formula that I discussed in Chapters 2 through 6. About two weeks after I had given out the tapes, one of the players, an extrovert, asked me if he could speak to me. When we met, he returned the tape with a comment: "It just doesn't seem to work for me. I play better when people give me shit." While I didn't give him exactly what he asked for, I did make another tape for him that combined positive imagery with some aggressive, challenging, confrontational comments.

Feeling-Oriented versus Thinking/Task-Oriented

Another personality style difference between players is that some are more task-oriented (T), while others are more feeling (F) and people-oriented. Feeling-oriented players are more social. They are concerned with how they feel, how others feel, and, of course, how others see and feel about them. They tend to play with passion and respond to a pat on the back. They appreciate people acknowledging them for who they are ("You are a good player," "You're someone I can really count on"). They are often upset when others say negative or uncomplimentary things about them.

Task-oriented players are primarily concerned with the task at hand — with analyzing what has to be done and doing it. They are less sensitive to general personal criticism and are more responsive to being acknowledged for a specific play or competency ("I liked the forecheck at the start of that shift, especially the way you went into the corner hard, pinned your man against the boards, and then got the puck").

Because of their task-based focus, "T" players may occasionally appear less emotional and less aware of — or sensitive to — the needs of the other players on the team. It is useful for players and coaches to be aware of these differences in perceptual style, that some players focus more on performing the specific tasks required by their position and role on the team, while others are more tuned in to the social aspects of participation in a team game. Again, it's important to understand who you are and to have the flexibility and balance to express your style in preparation and training.

Sensing versus Intuitive

Some players are more specific, "sensing," and detail-oriented (S) while others are more intuitive and are given to generalizing (N). The "S" players highlight differences. They can be exacting and they often focus on small imperfections. They enjoy creating and maintaining order. As part of their preparation they often break their jobs down into a series of specific tasks or elements ("If we are in their end with the puck, what I do is _____ , if they are in our end with the puck, what I do is _____ "), incorporating these elements into their mental rehearsals. They may give detailed consideration to how they will perform on each element. Sometimes they get too focused on detail and too upset with minor imperfections in their play. At those times they should be encouraged to step back, take a breath, and look at "the big picture" — that is, what the team is trying to accomplish.

Generalizers see the big picture. They read the overall pattern(s) of the game. However, they tend to pass over or skip detail. If you are coaching an "N," remember that he may benefit if you help him bring a sharper, more detailed focus to his perspective and imagery.

As we have said throughout, it is a good idea to go back to those days when you really excelled and reflect and run through what you did to prepare and perform on that day. If you go through the pregame preparation sheets, you will see that they encompass everything that you might do to prepare — from the time you get up and eat breakfast, to what you say to yourself between periods and after the game. Players who are more introverted, as well as those who are more task- and detail-oriented, are more likely to approach this evaluation with some interest. Their reports are apt to be more thorough. It's more difficult to encourage extroverts to fill in these preparation sheets or to keep a training journal.

While few hockey players seem to do it, keeping a journal can be a useful aid to the performance process. With good journal notes you can always go back and answer the questions, "What did I do [or not do] on that day I really played great?" You have a personal record of it. It's like a feedback or debriefing process. An elite youth team I worked with began keeping journals at the start of the season. The coach asked all the players to write down their goals, the skills to be improved, and what and how they prepared for each game. He felt it was a process that really helped his players be more focused, accountable, response-able, and effective. I'll describe their program in Chapter 13.

External Focus versus Internal Focus

The fourth area in which personalities are different is in focusing style. Some players focus more on externals, while others focus more internally. Externally focused players attend more to their surroundings — circumstances in the game, the rink, the crowd, their teammates — and will tend to pay less attention to how they feel and what's going on inside them. Externally focused players are often not aware of when and how to pump themselves up or calm down.

On the other side of the coin are those players who are more internally oriented. They have a clear idea of how they feel, but they may be less aware of what is going on in the game around them.

Whether internal or external, a player's degree of focus can vary between broad and narrow. A player with too broad an external focus may be easily distracted and display a tendency to react to everything going on around him. Players with a narrow internal focus are inclined to become overly self-reflective and excessively focused on their anxieties, aches, and pains. A player's focusing style can affect how he reads the game, how he manages himself, and how well he accepts coaching.[1]

Coaching Differences

A successful coach is one who responds to the challenge of understanding the marked range of personalities his players display. Of course, the same style differences that exist among players can also be found among coaches. Coaches can be introverted or extroverted, feeling- or task-oriented, detail people or generalizers, and internally or externally focused. An effective coach is one who knows his predispositions and can understand and relate to athletes of all styles.

---

1 For more information on focusing style, see the Test of Attentional and Interpersonal Style (TAIS), developed by Robert Nideffer and distributed by Enhanced Perfomance Systems.

A coach's personality style can affect the way he interacts with his players. For example, an extroverted coach may more readily understand the needs of extroverted players — what makes them tick and how to fire them up. However, to be more effective, the extroverted coach must adjust an energized and sometimes "in your face" style to the more sensitive personality of the introverted athlete. The Jones example I described earlier in this chapter illustrates how personality mismatches can be counterproductive. An extroverted coach may appreciate an extroverted player's appetite for input, spontaneity, and even confrontation. But there may be times when he's challenged to impose the order and structure necessary for an extroverted athlete.

Conversely, an introverted coach has some of the same "control preferences" as an introverted athlete and he may be challenged to display the necessary fire and flexibility to deal with a more outgoing, spontaneous, extroverted athlete.

The very analytical, task-oriented coach will have a greater understanding and ability to communicate with task-oriented athletes and is more challenged to give encouraging, emotional support to the feeling-type player. A coach who is more detail-oriented may find it an effort not to be too meticulous while still helping generalizers appreciate the value of precision in their preparation.

Whenever there are differences in personality or communication style between player and coach, both parties would be well advised to take a breath or two and exercise a little more patience and flexibility.

Again, whether you are a coach or a player, the idea is to assess and adjust. Get in touch with who you are and learn how to create the feelings and thoughts that help you get into your optimal zone. Clearly, differing personality styles do this in different ways. And there are different ways to coach players to help them to perform at their best.

Cliff Ronning, a veteran of the NHL wars and coaching styles, said, "If I were coaching I would try to be aware that every player has his own mind. It's important to know your players. Some are more sensitive than others. It's important to work with each individual. For example, introverts and extroverts are different. Some players need to calm down and others need to pump up. As a coach I would try to help my players learn and do what they need to know to be better."

Minnesota Wild captain Darby Hendrickson agrees: "You can't treat everyone the same. Players and circumstances are different. I think coaching is most effective when it has an awareness of those differences and a feel for what's needed in the moment."

Europeans have recently made inroads as head coaches in the NHL, and in some cases they have brought a different coaching style with them. One example is Alpo Suhonen, the Finnish-born former head coach of the Chicago Blackhawks. Tony Amonte, the Blackhawks' high-scoring winger, said of Suhonen, "He doesn't act like a North American coach. He never gets upset. It's different for the guys. He expects a lot out of his players. You're not having a coach telling you you're playing badly. The onus is upon yourself to know you're playing badly and to do something about it."[2]

A reporter asked Alpo whether everybody could handle that kind of responsibility, suggesting that some people need a firm hand on their shoulders and a coach breathing fire down their necks. Alpo's response was "What you right now are saying is very bad. You're saying only people are capable of handling the responsibility if somebody is yelling. That's very dangerous. Then they'll never learn to be responsible. If their father is yelling, teacher is yelling, coach is yelling, everybody's yelling — what kind of life is that? If you work in your office, the bosses don't yell at you, and still you do your work. Why do we treat sport differently? We don't do that in Europe."[3]

A veteran NHL winger bothered by his coach's yelling and swearing remarked, "Does he really think calling us dumb f— helps us play better?"

The complete player knows himself and is willing and able to adjust to any coaching style.

---

2 Jim Morrissey, "Red-hot Hawks have a cool, calm coach to thank,"
Chicago Tribune, January 18, 2001.
3 Ibid.

Change and Experience

Another aspect of individual difference to consider relates to the concept of change. Just as a child evolves and matures as a result of life experience, so a hockey player evolves through his experience of competition and training. What might have been useful at one stage of preparation may no longer be useful, or may be of less value, at a later phase.

Things change. For a rookie, being called up to play in a big game or in the playoffs is often a source of great excitement (even over-arousal) as the challenge to perform at a new and greater level of competition presents itself. To manage that anxiety, a rookie could benefit from doing some relaxing and breathing, and possibly some mental rehearsal and positive self-talk to prepare for the game. After that same player has racked up several years of experience, his view of the game may be very different. What had once been very exciting may now be just another game. Now, instead of calming down, the same player may actually have to focus on pumping himself up to get into his optimal zone.

Over the past couple of years, several NHL teams have carried out team-building workshops with their players. Part of the exercise involves exploring the personality style differences that exist between players. One workshop I participated in used a different way of categorizing players. Players were asked to evaluate themselves as to whether they were analyzers or riskers, practical or theoretical, independent or dependent.[4]

Analyzers are people or players who attempt to think things through before they act. They look, understand, and evaluate before they leap. Riskers, on the other hand, are players who tend to learn by experience. They often jump into a situation relatively unprepared and learn what to do — or not to do — by doing it. Coaches

4 For more information, see *Bi/Polar: Foundations of Productivity* by J.W. Thomas and T.J. Thomas (Austin, Texas: Institute of Foundational Training and Development, 1990).

seem to get more frustrated by a risker's seemingly impulsive and thoughtless action than by an analyzer's failure to act because he was thinking too much. There is some degree of correlation between riskers and extroverts, and analyzers and introverts. Interestingly, I'm told there are more analyzers than riskers in the NHL.

Another difference is that some players are dependent and some are independent. Both types can be leaders, it's just that their styles of leadership will be very different. The independent leader will decide on his own what to do and then say, "Let's go" or "Follow me." The more dependent leader will attempt to build consensus among the group before moving forward.

Lastly, there are practically minded players and theoretical types. The practical player tends to be interested in what to do and how to do it. The theoretical player has a greater interest in why it should be done. The detailed analysis and explanation that are often presented in coaching sessions run by a theoretical coach may seem long and boring to a practical player.

One piece of advice for coaches (especially those who fall into the more theoretical, analytical category) is not to provide an overabundance of analysis to players immediately before a game. It can get everyone thinking too much, and it's a turn-off for the following types: the practical, the risker, the extrovert, the generalizer, and the more instinctive/feeling player.

In the early 1980s I worked with two different head coaches on a successful NHL team. One was a good teacher and a strategist, a nice guy, and an intelligent, theoretically inclined coach. The other coach was also intelligent, but he was a practical fellow who could be sarcastic and who might get in your face. It fascinated me to watch different players react to these coaches. One player, a practical, risking, extroverted tough guy found the theoretical coach's teaching excessive and "demotivating." An introverted, theoretical, analytical defenseman found the same coach's technique excellent and he played his best hockey for that coach. By contrast, the former player excelled for the practical, confrontational coach, while the defenseman found him at times too callous and critical.

Vertical Thinkers versus Lateral Thinkers

Still another area of personality difference has to do with thinking style. Some players are more vertical — they tend to be more ordered, follow instructions, and process one thing at a time. They do not like ambiguity or change. Others are more lateral, tending to be more adaptable and less order-bound. These players read situations and adjust more easily — valuable qualities when it comes to adjusting to new assignments and linemates or defensive partners.

Bob was a motivated, coachable, veteran NHL defenseman. He was a conscientious defender and good at rushing the puck. He was struggling with his game on a team that was finding it hard to win. He called me because he felt uncomfortable and was playing with less confidence than usual. "Most of the time I do the right things to prepare," he said, "but I still feel unsure of myself out there and I have one of the worst plus/minuses on the team. I should be happy about all the ice I'm getting; they even have me on the power play. But things are changing so much . . . I never know who I'm playing with and we always seem to be out of sync. I feel like I don't know who's going to do what out there."

I encouraged Bob to keep doing what he was doing to prepare (relaxation and mental rehearsal). Then I explained to his coach that Bob was a very vertical type of player. He performed at his best when things were consistent and structured. Bob was most effective when he knew who he was playing with and what his and his partner's roles were. Under those circumstances, he could be a very reliable, competent NHL defenseman. However, when there was little consistency and structure, he would have trouble adjusting and give less than his best.

Adam was another vertical thinker troubled by having to adjust. He was an experienced NHL winger who was being double-shifted and he had two different assignments on two different lines. He was a grinder on a checking line part of the time and a set-up man on a high-scoring line the rest of the time. He sought me out because he found the contrast confusing. "I don't know what my ABCs should be and it's really messing me up," he said.

While most players perform best with a clearly defined role and familiar partners and linemates, some vertical players are bothered by changing circumstances. Others can more easily blend into playing any position on any line and still be effective.

There is no good or bad, right or wrong personality style. There are just differences between people. Growing your understanding of these differences can help you to be a more complete player or coach.

"Big Guy-Easy Syndrome"

The last difference that I want to discuss is one I call the "Big Guy-Easy Syndrome." Not everyone is gifted with the same tools and personality style — and the same is true for size. One thing I have observed is that some large players, who were big early and used their size to be successful at the lower levels (bantam, midget, high school, and even junior) don't develop the same work ethic as their smaller counterparts — largely because they don't have to. If you're big, you can sometimes get the job done with your size alone, while the only way for a smaller player to succeed is to work hard and keep moving.

Consequently, some developmental coaches may be satisfied with less effort from the big men compared with what is demanded of the smaller players. This may lead to a tendency among the bigger players to be lazy. The key to helping these big guys increase their work output isn't simply to tell them to work harder. In some cases they actually have to be put on a structured program and shown what to do — and even have it modeled for them.

I have seen it in junior and the NHL, where some big guys do their thing and then cruise. Some don't seem to understand they have to give more. I remember one NHL prospect who had been a big star throughout his junior career. At the end of training camp he was surprised and annoyed to learn that he hadn't made the big-league team. "I worked harder this summer then I've ever worked before," he complained, as if working hard automatically should have entitled him to the reward of playing in the NHL. The truth is that he was an "easy" player who needed to train harder and work harder on the ice on every shift.

After training and playing a few games with the NHLers, he saw how hard everyone else was working and began to appreciate his need to make a greater effort, but it wasn't easy for him to adjust because he had developed some lazy habits that had become part of his identity. Indeed, several NHL coaches, including Scotty Bowman, have said that if a player completes his development without learning how to work hard — and be successful in the process — it can be difficult, if not impossible, for him to turn things around and become an effective, mentally tough player in the NHL.

HOMEWORK ⇒

There are three assignments for Chapter 7.

Assignment 1 ⇒

Reflect on your personality style.

Are you more of an extrovert or an introvert? _____

Are you more of a thinking person or a feeling person? _____

Are you more task-oriented or a generalizer? _____

Are you more internally or externally focused? _____

Are you more likely to be broad or narrow in focus? _____

Most people have elements of both extremes in their personalities. If one is clearly more outstanding, then review the game preparation sheet and consider what adjustments you will need to make in your game preparation as a function of who you are.

Assignment 2 ⇒

Fill in the game preparation sheet for your next three or four games and review the input.

Assignment 3 [Optional] ⇒

Try keeping a journal for the next month.

Chapter 8

Teamwork Makes Winning Teams

Hockey is the ultimate team game. I have worked with teams in the National Hockey League, National Football League, National Basketball Association, and in Major League Baseball, and in my opinion players on a good hockey team are closer and more interdependent during the game than those in any of the other major sports. Part of the reason is the nature of the game. Hockey is a lateral, fluid game. Success in hockey comes from everyone working together and moving the puck from player to player. Moving the puck is what generates scoring opportunities.

I've heard a story about Roger Neilson lining his players up along the blue line in practice and telling the players on each line to skate as fast as they could to the far end of the rink. When he gave the signal, the first line sprinted down the ice as fast as they could. When they had reached the far blue line, Roger fired a puck at the end boards. The puck beat the players across the goal line. He repeated the process with the second line; they took off at full speed, and again, he fired the puck the minute they gained the blue line. Again the puck beat the players to the end boards. No matter how many times he ran the drill, no matter how hard the skaters tried, the puck always got there first. Finally the players asked Roger, "What's the point? The puck's always going to get there first."

"Exactly," Neilson replied. "The puck always travels faster than you can skate. If you want to make something happen, *pass the puck.*"

What is a team? The definition I like best is that a team is a group of animals hitched together, pulling in a common direction to a common goal — like a dog team or a team of horses. Seen in this manner it's dramatically clear that if one of the dogs or horses stops pulling or pulls in another direction, he forces the rest of the team to pull harder.

Success in hockey comes about from everyone pulling together. It's about players understanding their roles, working together, executing the game plan, and respecting and supporting each other.

In hockey, the "we" must be greater than the "me." It is a significant challenge for a coach to mold and direct a diverse and talented collection of individuals with differing wants, goals, and personality styles into a working team. It is no less of a challenge for players to surrender their egos and individuality for the team's good. However, that's what it takes to win.

Great Coaches on Winning Teams

With an incredible 1,193 regular-season wins (including the 2000–2001 season) and eight Stanley Cup championships to his credit, Scotty Bowman is easily the winningest coach in NHL history. He said, "One of the greatest challenges for a coach is molding a group of players to play together and to depend on each other. No player can stand alone. It's hard for one guy, even a great player, to do it by himself — even two good players. It's hard to have all the pressure on a couple of guys. Anaheim, for example, has two very good players [Paul Kariya and Teemu Selanne, who was later traded to San Jose]. But two players can be stopped."

Success in hockey requires that all six players on the ice are working together. Scotty went on to say, "The team concept is very important. A team has got to have some kind of identity." Two key ingredients that Scotty identifies as critical to team success are that the players know their jobs and that there is a collective willingness to work hard. Scotty added that it is important that the better players on the team perceive themselves as stronger when they play together and model an excellent work ethic.

Phil Jackson, who has won multiple NBA championships as coach of the Chicago Bulls and the Los Angeles Lakers, wrote something similar about winning in his book, *Sacred Hoops.* Jackson mused that the Bulls became a championship team when Michael Jordan realized (with Jackson's help) that the great player is the one who makes the players around him better. A team can only succeed when everyone is committed to playing the team game.[1]

Vince Lombardi, the legendary and often-quoted NFL coach, was asked by Lee Iacocca, a great corporate leader, what he thought were the keys to a winning team. His answer is as true for hockey as for football. According to Lombardi, three things that make a winning team are:

The players have to know their jobs. In hockey, that means the players know what to do on the ice. They know the system, the game plan, their role, and their ABCs.

The "we" is bigger than the "me." Again, hockey is the ultimate team game. To win, players have to be willing to commit to serving the team and executing the team's game plan as opposed to their own agendas.

---

1 Phil Jackson and Hugh Delehanty, *Sacred Hoops* (New York: Hyperion, 1995).

The players must love one another. Lombardi went on to say that the reason the Green Bay Packers were NFL champions in the late 1960s was because the players loved one another.[2] When I relate this to players, I sometimes get a strange response. Lombardi didn't mean that the players had to like one another. He meant that the players had to respect each other, stand up for each other, and maintain a standard of play that reflected that respect.

Respect is the winger going hard into the corner and winning the puck so that he can feed it to the center, who is fighting for position in the front of the net. It's the defenseman blocking shots or fighting to clear the front of the net to give the goalie a better chance to see and stop the puck. When the shared vision of the team is that we all work the plan and give 100 percent on each and every shift, the team is successful.

Scott Mellanby is a veteran of 15 NHL seasons, during which he has been a 30-goal scorer, a team captain, and above all a team player. When I asked him what constituted a winning team, Scott reiterated what Jackson, Lombardi, and Bowman said: "Hockey is a team game and you simply can't win with one or two players. I've been to the Stanley Cup finals with two different teams. In both cases we had a strong leadership group of five or six guys who could have been captains. You must have a core of character guys."

When we discussed Phil Jackson's assertion that the great player is the one who makes the players around them better, Scott agreed: "Respect is vital. I've been an all-star and a fourth-liner. I know how it feels when the stars and first-line players respect the third- and fourth-line guys and make them feel an important part of the team. And it's those third- and fourth-line guys that have to score for you in the playoffs for you to win. If your top guys believe in those players, it will be easier for the team to believe in itself."

Scott mentioned that there are times in practice when a star and a fourth-liner will be teamed up together on a two-on-one drill. He said it's essential for the star to convey a positive attitude, make the

---

2 Quoted in *Iacocca: An Autobiography* by Lee A. Iacocca with William Novak (New York: Bantam, 1984).

fourth-liner feel that the star believes in his ability and is willing to work hard with him. "I have seen first-liners who do just that, and then there are those 'head hangers' who send the message, 'You're not good enough to drill with me.' And that kind of thing has a real negative impact on a team.

"A team needs character guys, and a player's true character emerges in the hard times. It's easy to be a good guy when things are going your way."

I am reminded of Mike Keenan's description of the Canada Cup–winning team he coached in 1991. Part of the reason for the team's success was that the players (all of whom were NHL stars) were remarkably supportive toward each other. "It was something you could feel when you walked into the room," Mike said.

Making a Difference through Effort

Another statement by Vince Lombardi that applies to hockey as well as football is about effort. Lombardi said that there are 50 to 60 plays in a football game, but only three or four are game-breakers that determine the outcome of the game. He said you must approach every play as if it's the one that is going to make the difference. It's the same in hockey. A player may have 20 or 30 shifts in a game, and maybe one or two of them will be game-breakers. You still have to play as if each and every shift is going to make the difference.

There's an old saying that goes, "On a team, everyone makes a difference." The question I often ask players is "What kind of a difference do you make? Will it be one that adds to the team, or one that detracts from it? It's your choice." The complete player is a team player.

Commitment and Teamwork

When the Vancouver Canucks held training camp in Kamloops, British Columbia — home of the Western Hockey League Blazers, who won the Memorial Cup three times in the 1990s — I noticed some advice posted on the wall of the home team's dressing room. It was called "The Blazers' Code of Commitment" and it read as follows:

- *To prepare every day as best we can*
- *To play with discipline every shift*
- *To support each other every shift*
- *To never let ourselves be outworked*
- *To follow the game plan to the best of our ability*
- *To pay the price necessary to win*

These are team directives designed to help individuals play as a team and win at a team game. One more Blazers tidbit: also on the door of their dressing room is a sign that reads, "The name on the front of the jersey is more important then the one on the back."

Building a Winning Team

Pat Quinn has been the NHL's coach of the year with two different teams. When I asked Pat how you go about building a winning team, he said, "You begin with what you've got. If possible, you set up a model with strength down the middle. It starts in goal. Good goaltending creates confidence for the people up front. Center is the key position to the transition game. No team wins the Cup without strength at center."

Speaking of strength at center, Mark Messier has won the Stanley Cup six times with two different teams, the Edmonton Oilers and the New York Rangers. He says, "You need good players to win, but winning is more than that. There's a certain kind of feeling, an expectation of success, that's part of a winning team.

"It develops on different teams for different reasons. On some teams, there's so much talent and skill that you just know you're good — and that you can and will be successful. The Edmonton Oilers were like that, and it was fun to be a part of that." When he compares Edmonton to the New York team he captained to the championship, Mark says the experience and strong feeling of leadership on the Rangers created a positivity and confidence that permeated the room and the team. "On other teams without as much talent and experience, a certain belief in the team comes about by working hard together. You can create a winning mindset by playing a solid team game.

"It's important that all the players believe that they contribute and that they make a difference. Whether a guy plays 30 minutes or five minutes, whether he's a scorer or a checker, when everyone believes he makes a difference, and plays like he makes a difference, remarkable things can happen. I've seen it."

I asked Marc Crawford, who coached the Colorado Avalanche to a Stanley Cup title, about the process of building a winning team. Marc's answer can be applied to developing a winning team as well as a winning player. "First, you have to assess what you've got in terms of talent and character. You have to become aware of your strengths and deficiencies, and build from there. If there is a void in an area — whether it's talent, character, or leadership — the void must be filled, and the talent you have must be developed." When I asked Marc about the developmental process, he said, "You have to instruct your players. We do it by talking with them and using video to increase their awareness, their sense of responsibility, and confidence. Lastly, you have to provide some feedback to the players on how they are doing. This feedback should be more positive than negative."

It's the same in becoming a more complete player. To develop, a player must assess where he is, become aware of his strengths and deficiencies, and then adjust. He does that by setting goals based on the skills and strengths he wants to develop, then working hard. A positive focus is important when developing skills. That involves using positive self-talk and positive imagery (described in chapters 3 and 4). Lastly, a player must reflect and critique (reassess) his on-ice performance, acknowledging his successes as well as the things he must improve.

Improving Teamwork

What can you as a player do to improve teamwork?

First of all, know your job. If you are not clear, ask the coaches. Understand what your linemates or defensive partners think and expect.

Second, communicate. Have a clear positive focus of what you want to do on the ice (clear ABCs), and the players around you will respond to your focus and action. For example, if the center knows that a winger will work hard in the corner to win the puck and then pass it to the front of the net, the center will do what is necessary to get to the front of the net and make the play. Similarly, if the winger knows the center will work hard to be free in front, he will work hard to get the puck to him. Talk with your teammates. Each person being clear about what he has to do, and working to do it, will affect his teammates. Encourage and acknowledge the positive effort of your teammates.

Winning teams are about a commitment to team play, to the game plan, and to each other. Model a winning attitude. Work hard in practice to improve your skills, to bring a high quality and tempo to drills, and to model a winning work ethic.

Lastly, improve your conditioning so that you can keep executing — shift after shift, game after game.

To play hockey well you must surrender the "me" for the greater "we." When the game is played at its best, you will get back more than what you give up, plus you will have the satisfaction of being a part of something greater than yourself. A quote from Mark Messier posted on the wall of the WHL Kelowna Rockets' dressing room reminds the players of just this point: "If everybody can find a way to put their personal agendas aside for the benefit of the team, ultimately they will gain for themselves in the long run. But I think what often happens is people think they have to take care of themselves first and the team second. Then the infrastructure breaks down and nobody's accountable. You have to sacrifice yourself for the good of the team, no matter what role you play on the team — whether you're playing 30 minutes or two minutes a game."

Be Prepared

According to coach Roger Neilson, one of the qualities necessary to being a star player, one which is sometimes overlooked, is consistency. And Roger feels preparation is the key to being consistent. He says one of the most important things to learn is how to get yourself ready to play, day after day, game in and game out, throughout a long season. When I asked Roger how a player might go about doing that, he said, "If a team has a hockey system, the coach's task is to get the players to play the system. Playing the system creates order, and that provides consistency. The same is true on a personal preparation level. It's having your own system and knowing what you have to do to execute on the ice and focusing on that. It's also knowing how to prepare for games and running your routine, day after day throughout the season."

Preparation is a key to confidence and success. Throughout this book there are suggestions on how to prepare. Let's review five things you can do to prepare.

First, set a goal — or goals — for what you want to do on the ice and in the gym. When you step onto the ice for practice, think, "Today, I'm really going to work on _____, or to make _____ happen."

Train your weaknesses and play your strengths. Most players like to look good. Consequently, they tend to practice what they are good at and are less inclined to work on some of their weaker qualities. An experienced junior coach like Gary Davidson will tell you that the players who stand out are consistently those who set goals and work hard to make themselves better by working on their weaknesses as well as their strengths. Gary coached the Kariya brothers in the British Columbia Hockey League, and he has said that two things that set Paul and Steve Kariya apart from the others were their ability to identify the things they had to improve on and their remarkable willingness to work on their weaknesses.

I asked Steve Kariya about what Gary's assessment, and he replied: "If you want to play in the NHL, you have to develop all your abilities, the whole package. And to do that you have to practice the things you are not good at. There are guys in junior who just keep taking those big slap shots in practice . . . [they're working on a skill] that they rarely have the time and space to use in the NHL."

Gary also pointed out that the Kariyas were positive and practical. They didn't dwell on things they couldn't control, like their lack of size. Instead, they maximized their quickness and strength. Gary recalled the end of the first year in which he coached Paul Kariya as a junior. The 16-year-old asked him what he needed to work on to improve. Gary advised Paul to focus on his shot, specifically on developing his accuracy and a quick release. "I don't know how many thousands of shots he took over the summer," Gary says, "but when he came back in the fall it was clear he had dedicated himself to the task because Paul's shot was quicker, more accurate, and a lot more powerful." The fact that Paul has become a prolific goal scorer and is often among the league leaders in shots on goal is a testament to the value of commitment, talent, and hard work.

Larry Robinson, a Hall of Fame defenseman and a Stanley Cup–winning coach with the New Jersey Devils, made a similar point when I asked him how he would help a player develop. Larry said he would get the player to focus on his weaknesses, not his strengths. "Most athletes focus on their strengths. It's human nature to focus on what you're good at, and what comes easily to you. If it's easier to turn right, then people go to the right. In terms of their development, it's important to get them to do what they have trouble doing." He related an experience he had had with Paul Coffey when they played together for Team Canada in the 1984 Canada Cup tournament. "I noticed Paul always went to his right. I asked him about it and he said he never realized that he was doing it."

Donald Brashear also believes you have to work on things that challenge you. "There's a part of the game that comes naturally to me. That's being the enforcer and playing physical. I don't need to focus on that. I focus more on things that are harder for me. That way I improve on these things. The other things I know I'll do well."

Right Feelings and Preparation

Another thing you can do to prepare is learn to create the right feelings. Get in touch with who you are and the emotions — and emotional level — that facilitate your performance. Assess and adjust. If you tend to be too nervous, tense, or intense, learn how to calm yourself down. If you find there are times when you are flat, learn how to energize or pump yourself up. Reflect on your performance style and learn to do whatever is necessary to help yourself develop and excel as a player and teammate.

Mark was a hard-working junior defenseman who very much wanted to be a team player. Though he wasn't big, he was a fearless, physical player who would stand up to anyone to protect his teammates. The problem was, Mark didn't have control of his temper. In the second period of a close game, with his team leading 1–0, Mark was speared. He retaliated and was given a two-minute penalty. Not surprisingly, he was upset. Thirty seconds after Mark went into the penalty box, the other team scored a power-play goal. As Mark left the penalty box, still steaming, one of the opposing players skated by and said something to the effect that Mark was a dummy who'd just cost his team a goal. Mark snapped. He jumped the opponent and started throwing punches. When the smoke had cleared, Mark was back in the penalty box, all by himself, with a two-minute penalty for instigating the fight and a five-minute penalty for fighting. The complexion of the game shifted.

Clearly, it's not enough to care, to work hard, and to stand up for your teammates. The complete player is a team player, and that means playing smart hockey with self-control and not allowing your emotions (right brain) to override your focus (left brain).

Part of preparing yourself and creating right feelings is helping your body get what it needs. That means eating intelligently and getting enough quality rest. Choose foods that will energize you and help you perform well. Most experts recommend a pregame diet loaded with complex carbohydrates, with moderate protein. Avoid a pregame meal of empty junk food. One way to discover if there are certain foods that help or hinder your performance is to keep a record (in a performance journal) of what you eat and see if there is a relationship to your game performance. As far as rest is concerned, it's been said that "fatigue makes a coward of us all." Weariness certainly doesn't lead to consistent, high-level performance. When it comes to rest, use your common sense. If you are tired, take the time to rest and recharge.

＊

A third thing you can do to prepare yourself to play is to create clear focus. Understand the game plan and know what to do on the ice in a variety of game situations. If you have any uncertainties, discuss them with a coach. Go over your ABCs. And use mental rehearsal to see yourself performing well. With mental practice your reactions become more automatic.

I spoke to Chris Pronger of the St. Louis Blues about optimal pregame preparation. His response was sensible. He spoke about doing visualization and creating a positive frame of mind. "Preparation is a personal matter," Chris said. "Some players start preparing the morning of the game, others start in the afternoon, and still others don't prepare until right before the game. A player should find out what works for him, then do it before every game."

Along with imagery, be aware of your thinking. Be a positive self-talker. Remember to change the channel or park any negative thoughts. Stay on your positive-power channel. Before, during, and after the game, speak positively to yourself and your teammates. Acknowledge your ability and affirm your, and their, success.

＊

Work to strengthen your winning attitude. Remember your goals and your personal commitment to use everything to be a better player and a better person. Confidence grows with preparation. Know that you are physically and mentally prepared. Know that you have the energy, skill, and determination to execute your ABCs. (If not, work to improve your training program.) See yourself executing well. Know that's who you are. Reinforce your identity as someone who knows his job and can be counted on to make the play. Remember, hockey is a great game. It's a high-speed challenge on ice. Allow yourself to enjoy it.

Fifth, and finally, just do it.

HOMEWORK Ⅲ➡

There is only one homework assignment for Chapter 8.

Assignment 1 Ⅲ➡

Carefully consider (and list) the things you can do to be a better team player. Then do them and be it.

Introduction to Chapters 9 to 11

In the next three chapters we review the basics of feeling, focus, and attitude discussed in chapters 1 through 8 as they apply to three key performance areas: scoring, playing defense, and goaltending.

Each of these chapters incorporates the comments and insights of experienced NHL players and coaches who are or were experts in scoring, playing defense, and tending goal. The diversity of their experience and insights makes it clear that there is more than one way to prepare for and play the game. How you choose to prepare and play depends on who you are, what your role is on the team, and the challenge in front of you. To become a more complete player it's important to know yourself and observe and study others.

Chapter 9

Mental Tips on Playing Offense and Scoring

In Chapter 2, I presented a graph that showed the relationship between arousal and performance. If a player feels too tense, tight, or overaroused, his performance level can drop. Similarly, if a player is too laid-back or not sufficiently aggressive, performance will also suffer. I have seen both kinds of problems with scorers.

Most common is the scorer who feels too tight and is squeezing the stick — pressing or trying too hard. The best advice for him is to change his feelings and his focus. To do that, I recommend that the player release, breathe, and refocus. One of the reasons I emphasize working with breathing is that it has helped many players to manage their feelings effectively. Releasing and breathing can clear the mental TV screen of negative or high-pressure feelings and make it easier to focus on making the play and doing what you can to get the puck into the net. Those players who report they play more on instinct can often regain their touch just by letting go of the tension and tuning in to right feelings.

Dan was more of a checker than a scorer, but he did generate scoring chances and he wanted to be more effective at capitalizing on these chances when they were there for him. He felt he was always rushing himself around the net. He asked how he could develop the sense that he had more time. One suggestion was for him to focus on breathing — specifically rhythm. We did some training in which Dan would focus on smooth breathing, especially giving himself time for the in breath to come all the way in and the out breath to go all the way out. Then he would imagine (mentally rehearse) reacting smoothly, patiently, and effectively in a variety of scoring opportunities — in front of and around the net, getting a rebound, holding the puck, waiting that extra half second to see the opening, seeing it and scoring; making a short pass, going hard to the net, taking the pass, and flicking the puck into the net; circling into the slot, taking a pass, seeing the opening, and shooting accurately into the net.

I usually suggest that the scorer who is too tense and overaroused focus on being "smooth," and "like a star," and that he concentrate on affirmations like "good hands" or "one good shift at a time." The ABCs are another productive focus. Imagery is also a powerful, positive focus that can enhance scoring. The kind of imagery that I think is most beneficial is mental rehearsal. See yourself with great finish, getting open, having a hard, accurate shot, being quick, being lucky, and putting the puck in the net. Stimulating images can also be helpful. Being a panther or tiger, hunting and being as quick as a big cat — and strong in front of the net — can also help your scoring game.

There are also those players who would score more if they played a more aggressive, attacking, go-for-it brand of hockey. Some are simply underaroused and need to get fired up.

Jim was an NHL winger, a big guy who was dangerous when he went hard to the net — but he rarely did. It was possible for him to get fired up to the point that he could crash the net and score. But such episodes were infrequent — it usually took a cross-check or a slash to get him going. The problem was that Jim didn't know how to pump himself up. You must always assess and adjust. Know the right feelings for you to be at your best — and know how to create these feelings.

Many of the facets of attitude that I have discussed come into play in scoring. You have to be committed to work on the basics, including your ability to skate, pass, and shoot. You have to be committed to go to the net and stay in front, even when the lumber is heavy. You have to be confident, to believe you can score — go for it and be a shooter. It helps to feel as if you deserve it.

It's interesting to note that, when a scorer's confidence vanishes (and confidence can be fragile), it can significantly affect his physical game. Without confidence, scorers don't seem to get to the right place at the right time. They don't seem to win the one-on-one battles, and they can't seem to pull the trigger. It may be because of confidence, and perhaps also self-image, but many scorers have an almost egocentric or selfish attitude of "I'm the guy, give it to me." They want the puck. They believe they can score, and they e*xpect* good things to happen.

All kinds of players score goals. While scorers tend to be a little more "self-centered," there is no one single personality profile of a scorer. Extroverts score, and so do introverts. Task-oriented and feeling types can both be scorers. The interesting thing is that different types of adjustments must be made to help each of these types play and score effectively. As a coach, there are times to confront, to challenge, and to provide more structure for an extrovert. And calm and encourage the more introverted type of scorer. It may be helpful to watch tapes and analyze play with the task-oriented scorer, while on the other hand taking the time to support the feeling player before offering advice.

Another thing to be aware of is that analytical, "left-brained" players like to know and see what they have to do, and then be allowed to go out and do it. They find it helpful to review ABCs and do mental rehearsal. The more instinctive/feeling/"right-brained" players prefer not to think too much before games, although working with ABCs and imagery can still be helpful if used well in advance of a game.

I asked a few veteran NHL players with a gift for putting the puck in the net to offer up some mental tips on scoring. Whenever possible, I've tried to put their words and advice into the framework I've outlined in chapters 1 through 6.

Cliff Ronning is a scorer with whom I consulted for half a dozen years. At first, the critics said he was too small to play the game, but this NHL star has been almost a point-a-game player for 14 years. Some keys to his success are his on-ice intelligence and his commitment to physical and mental preparation.

"Scoring is all to do with timing," Cliff says. "It's about not being too quick, or too slow. It's arriving at the right time and being in control. You don't want to get too far ahead of the play."

"Focus is the key. You have to be focused on the play. I mean *really* focused, on the ice. Sometimes when I'm tuned in I see the ice surface as a series of little squares, or triangles — [and the game as] a series of potential two-on-ones."

As Cliff describes it, scoring is a balance between being aggressive, being tuned in and focused, anticipating the play and making things happen, while still being in the moment and able to react.

Cliff has also found the idea of "good hands, good wheels, good eyes" useful. His ABCs include:

A. Be alert.
B. Make good passes, tape to tape.
C. Jump up into the hole.
D. Want to receive the puck.
E. Be in control and aware of what's around you.

F. Be confident with the puck. Be confident enough to hang onto the puck for a split second longer and take an extra second to make the play. Many scorers have that ability to stay calm under pressure and be comfortable holding the puck for that extra half second that increases their on-ice intelligence and scoring possibilities.

G. Shoot hard. If you want the puck to go in, visualize it going into the net.

Don't just send a "hoper" at the net. Shoot with intention. Make it happen. See the holes. "I don't even look or know where the goalie is," Cliff says. "I just see mesh. Remember, you have to shoot to score. Get the puck at the net."

Pavel Bure, one of the most exciting scorers in the game, says, "I always try to read the game and the flow of the puck. Anticipating a turnover and where the puck may go is critical to getting a good jump. For example, when a defenseman is about to shoot the puck, I see where he is shooting from and I anticipate where the puck will go. I want to know how it will come off the boards, [so I can] move to that spot on the blue line with the shot. In hockey you have to continuously read the game and react."

Pavel, "the Russian Rocket," is famous for his electrifying break-aways. I asked him if he had a focus on breakaways. He laughed and said, "Yeah, it's to get away from the guy behind me." As for his focus regarding the net and where he is going to shoot, he said, "It's a feeling thing . . . I don't think about where I'm going to shoot. It's an automatic reaction between mind and body. It's just making a move I've practiced thousands of times."

For a young player who has good hands and good wheels and wants to develop his offensive potential, Pavel says, "The only advice I have is pretty general: work hard."

When it comes to pregame preparation, Pavel said rest is a key element for him. When I asked him if he does any specific mental preparation before games, he said, "No. To be honest, the less I think about the game the better."

A teammate of Pavel's once described him as "one of the most competitive guys I ever played with." So I asked him about self-talk and whether there were any specific things he said to himself during the game to maintain his intensity and focus. "What I say to myself most often during the game is, 'Don't get frustrated.'" The topic of frustration led me to ask him how he dealt with being held or slashed by an opposing player. Without hesitating, Pavel replied, "If I get slashed by someone, I slash him back, right away. Then I forget about it."

It's not exactly the advice I offered when I discussed mental toughness in Chapter 6, but I guess it works for Pavel.

Alexander Mogilny of the Toronto Maple Leafs is another talented scorer with a practical intelligence for the game. Over his 12-year NHL career, Mogilny has scored nearly 400 goals, including 76 in one season with the Buffalo Sabres. I asked him if the hockey program in the former Soviet Union made use of sport psychology. He said that, if so, he had had no exposure to it. I also asked him the same question I asked of Bure: If he were coaching a talented young hockey player, is there something he might be able to offer the player to help him become a better scorer?

"No, I don't think so," Alex said. "I think it's just something you are born with. You either have it or you don't." I approached him with the question on another occasion, and again he demurred. Finally, after I persisted, he said, "Okay, okay. The only thing I can say is, if you want to score you have to shoot the puck. Shoot the puck at the net."

Paul Kariya is an NHL all-star winger who has used his intelligence, speed, and excellent shot to become a prolific scorer. Here are his ABCs for scoring:

   A. You have to shoot the puck to score.
   B. You have to get your shot away quick and shoot on the net.

"I'm not always trying to hit a specific spot," Paul explained. "Sometimes I don't know exactly where a shot is going to go. I may be thinking of a spot. The goalie may even be sensing the same spot. The shot may not go exactly where I wanted it to, yet it still beats him. To score, you've got to shoot the puck, shoot it quick, and shoot it on net."

   C. Get into a good scoring position.

"That might be the high slot for me, or in front of the net for a power forward," Paul says. "You don't score many goals from the corner."

   I asked Paul if there were specific things he said to himself during the game to keep focused. "I am a believer in positive, constructive thinking," he said. "But I don't like to think too much during the game. It's important to be in the moment. As Yogi Berra said, 'How can you think and hit at the same time?' Sometimes during the game I may remind myself to get my focus back. Or if something upsets me, I'll tell myself to 'park it.' But I believe a key to performing well is not to think too much and to stay in the moment."

Mark Messier told me, "I'm not the right guy to ask about scoring goals." I protested that, since he has netted more than 600 of them in NHL regular-season play, and another 100 in the playoffs, he might just be qualified to speak about scoring.

   "Well," he replied, "my focus has never just been scoring, it's been winning — and doing whatever had to be done to win. There's a difference. Had I been a pure scorer, someone like Mike Bossy, I may have been able to score more goals. But I varied what I did depending on the needs of the team. Sometimes it was scoring, sometimes it was playing a more defensive role, and sometimes it was being more of a team leader." Clearly, there's a difference between being a pure scorer and an all-around team player.

Wayne Gretzky has confirmed what his former teammate says, and offered this assesment of Mark's motivation and focus: "The measure of Mark's game is not in goals and assists. The statistic he cares about is the number of Stanley Cups won."

Mark shared the following observations about scoring: "I think one of the biggest changes in hockey over the last 20 years has been in goaltending. The equipment is better and goalies are better technically. I think it's harder to score. It used to be that when you would skate down the wing, the goalie would play tight on the near post and not come out or cut off the angle. You could actually see space between the goalie and the far post, and if you made that shot you would score."

"But you still score from the wing," I told him, then asked about his patented wrist shot, which he takes off his back foot as he's coming down the wing. "How is it that that shot is so effective?"

"I come down the wing with speed, and just before I shoot I move laterally as well as toward the net. That causes the goalie to adjust. Sometimes I am able to catch the goalie moving. When I can do that, there are some openings and he can be beaten."

Mark expressed some definite views about the importance of preparation that relate to every phase of the game, including scoring. "Preparation begins well before a player gets to the rink the night of a game," he says. "Over the summer months, before the season starts, you build strength. Today in professional sport, with so many games and so much travel, you really have to learn how to build strength and stay in great shape to be effective. Every team has experts with good strength and conditioning programs. Some players follow them. How you feel affects how you think and play. When you are weak and tired you feel more vulnerable and less confident. When you are strong you feel more confident and more like you can make a difference.

"Game preparation should begin before you get to the rink. A lot of things go into it — thinking about the game, watching what other teams and other players do, and seeing what you can learn from that. Getting the right amount of rest, eating right, and having positive self-talk are all important parts of preparation. A lot of players don't know anything about self-talk. They don't realize that saying negative things to themselves, even when they are not playing, can lead to more negative play.

"It's important for a team to have some time just before the game to bring their energy together. After team meetings and [after the players have spent some time] in the training room and adjusting their equipment, I like to see everybody in the room with the music off an hour before game time. That time together is special. It doesn't always have to be the guys talking about the game — sometimes there's humor. But it's the guys talking together and coming together as a team. That's very important."

Luc Robitaille, now with the Detroit Red Wings, has scored so frequently over the course of his 15 NHL seasons (nearly 600 regular-season goals and more than 1,200 points) that he's called "Lucky." Having known Luc since his first season with the Los Angeles Kings, I can say that he's a nice guy and it has been a pleasure to watch him evolve into one of the league's top scorers.

Luc is an instinctive/feeling type of player and he generously shares his ideas about focus and preparation. "After a shift, I never think back about things I missed on the ice," he says. "That's in the past. Instead, I focus on what's happening now. I see where people are getting open. I see where the puck should go. It's important to watch and be aware.

"When I played with Gretzky, I noticed he watched everything. He was very aware. He could tell you who had scored and assisted on all the goals. And if a player was injured, Wayne was the first guy onto the ice to replace him. Of course, the more you play, the more you pick up. I watch the other guys to see what I can learn."

About preparation, Luc says, "Work hard in practice. Practice the system. You must know where you should be on the ice. And you must work out, have good nutrition, and rest."

Beyond that, Luc says, do whatever works for you. "Everybody has their own way to get ready. The easier you make it for yourself, the better. Some players are too inflexible about their preparation routine. I'm not. Before the game, we get information about the other teams on paper. I look it over, but I don't like to worry too much about it. I really like to be at ease with my mind. The less I think about the game, the better off I am. I produce on instinct. I find when I think too much about what I should be doing, I get behind." (In that respect Luc's comments are similar to those of Pavel Bure.)

When it comes to visualization, Luc has this to say: "I do some from time to time. But I find that when I visualize myself scoring I think about it too much and it slows me down." He continues, "Hockey is different than the other sports. There are no set plays in hockey. There are no free throws or patterns that you can visualize exactly as they'll take place. Hockey is all about reaction — everything happens because of someone else's mistakes. You have to be able to react. And you have to be creative to score."

I mentioned to Luc that many players used some form of visualization. "I think visualization is more useful for a defensive player," Luc says. "Defense is more of a set game. They are playing more of a system, and more one-on-one. But to put the puck in the net, you must be creative."

Clearly, Luc knows what works for him. Of course, mentally rehearsing yourself taking a pass and beating the goalie can be effective preparation. Remember the concept of scoring 50 goals a day. It works.

I asked Luc what he could do to help a young player with good skills become a better player and a better scorer. His reply: "I would teach him the basics of the game. And then I would watch and see if he practices them, and whether he was willing to work hard. I would decide whether he really loves to play hockey. People can help, but it's got to be up to you." Like Pavel Bure and Mark Messier,

Luc believes that, to be successful, you've got to work hard and love the game. If you do, you might get lucky.

There are a lot of theories as to what made Wayne Gretzky such a great scorer. Some people said it was his ability to see the ice, to anticipate, to read patterns, and to innovate. Others praised his remarkable stick skills and his aerobic capacity. I mentioned earlier that in 1986 — when Gretzky was at his best — Rick Lanz, who was then a young defenseman, spoke about Gretzky's remarkable ability to hold the puck. "He makes me make the first move." Recently, when we were discussing scoring, Rick made another point: "People like Gretzky and Ronning are very comfortable on their skates. Moving on ice is second nature to them, and consequently they are free to concentrate totally on puck movement. Many other players have to focus on just getting there, but Gretzky's focus was entirely on the play."

A key question, of course, is whether this ability to be cool under pressure, to hold the puck that extra half second and then execute effectively, can be taught. I believe it can, at least to some extent. There are five training areas that I think could improve a player's ability to be calm under pressure and execute well.

First of all, the player must improve his skating ability so that skating becomes second nature and therefore one less something to think about. If a player doesn't have to focus on skating, he's free to focus more on the puck.

Next, the player has to work on managing his emotions so that he goes to the net aggressively while at the same time remaining cool under pressure. That involves breathing, releasing, and being a star, which we discussed at length in Chapter 2.

I can't stress enough the importance of doing some mental rehearsal. I believe it can be useful to visualize shooting and scoring in pressure-filled situations. Imagine yourself being calm, handling the puck, making and receiving passes, and finishing.

Another key is to learn to read patterns of puck flow so that, like

Pavel Bure or Wayne Gretzky, you can anticipate where the puck is going and be one step ahead. The earlier a young player is taught or encouraged to train himself to read the game, the more it can influence his complete development as a player. Psychologists have observed that early experience shapes later learning. In some cases, it even influences neuroanatomy.

Finally, it's essential to combine your imagery with actual on-ice practice to improve stick skills — passing, shooting, stickhandling — and keeping your head up (so that you can see what's happening instead of looking down at the puck). By practicing your stick skills and developing your shot and your goal-scoring reflex you will maximize on the scoring opportunities you generate through hard work.

Scoring is the result of doing the basics well and maintaining a positive mindset. Instead of worrying about the end result, work on the basics. Do the mental and physical training. Create right feelings and right focus. See yourself performing well. Remember, confidence comes from preparation as well as success.

Chapter 10

Mental Tips on Playing Defense

Playing good defense involves the same basics of right focus and right feelings described in chapters 1 through 8. The only difference is that some people believe that defense may be the most difficult position in hockey to play.

Playing good defense requires a diversity of skills. A defenseman has to have game smarts, strength, mobility, and reliable hands. A defenseman has more responsibilities and must make more consequential reads than forwards do. A defenseman must have more agility and physical strength than the goalie. If a defenseman fails to tie up a 220-pound center in front of the net or gets beaten one-on-one by a speedy winger, the consequences can be embarrassing and costly. All of which means the position is a greater challenge to play. It's not surprising, therefore, that defensemen mature more slowly than forwards — indeed, many NHL defensemen are not truly comfortable and confident about playing their position until they are in their mid to late twenties.

The keys to playing effectively on defense are good eyes, good wheels, and good hands. As I've mentioned, strength also helps. By good eyes, I mean good vision, especially good peripheral vision. One of the keys that every defenseman I have spoken with has articulated is the need to make good reads. By that they mean being aware of who is on the ice and where, and knowing what is happening and what could possibly happen next. Playing good defense when the other team has the puck is about anticipating their play and maintaining good position. Playing good defense when your team has the puck requires you to be aware of when and where to move the puck, when to jump into the play, and to do it all quickly and with confidence. Awareness and timing are critical, both in regard to reading opportunities and reacting at the right instant, whether it's gapping up properly (judging and matching your speed to the forward's speed) or stepping up and supporting the rush.

Bret Hedican, a speedy defenseman with the Florida Panthers, says, "The speed of the play in the NHL is so fast that you have to know who's on the ice and where they are, so that you can anticipate and react almost before things happen." Bret went on to say that one of the real challenges facing the young defenseman is to constantly remind himself to be aware of what's going on and not just react and chase the puck.

Larry Robinson, who twice won the Norris Trophy as the NHL's premier blue-liner, offers similar advice on the importance of being aware of what's happening around you. "A lot of kids are mesmerized by the puck," Larry says. "You have to look and read so you won't be surprised. Be aware. It's very important for a defenseman to know what to do before you get the puck. Know what's happening. Know who's coming at you. Know if you have time. Communication is also important. Talk out loud.

"If I'm the guy carrying the puck, I might communicate to move a player. If someone's about to hit one of our players, I'd tell him to look out. I also used to talk to myself on the ice, to keep myself focused."

Mark Hardy, a veteran of 19 pro seasons who is now an assistant coach for the Los Angeles Kings, concurs. "For me, the most important things about playing defense were being in control and being consistent. I wanted to control my intensity and to stay focused on doing the four or five basic things that I knew I had to do well."

Like good eyes, good wheels are an asset to all players. For a defenseman, good wheels are fundamental to reading and reacting to the play. Superior skating ability can allow you to make things happen and to recover if you are caught in the wrong position.

Mattias Ohlund, one of the NHL's better young defensemen, explained that if a defenseman isn't skating well and is slow to the puck, he has less time to read the play and less opportunity to make good decisions. Defensemen who labor with their skating frequently find themselves struggling to catch up to the play and under pressure to react. Often they are forced to move the puck without a heads-up read of the situation.

If you are an aggressive forward, be aware that pressuring the forecheck means that the defense has less time to break out and start the rush. That usually generates poorer decisions and more mistakes, especially for less mobile and less composed defensemen.

Good hands are a gift for a forward, but they're a must for a defenseman. Mishandling the puck in your end can be a disaster. Sure hands on defense reduce everybody's anxiety. By good hands I mean owning or protecting the puck, being able to take and make a pass, and controlling the puck at the point. A hard, accurate point shot is desirable, but remember that accuracy, which is an expression of control, is more important than just shooting hard.

Essentially, there are two styles of playing defense. D1 is the classic, stay-at-home defenseman. D1 tends to be a more physical player and is able to control or clear the area in front of the net and move the puck forward. His core game is his solid, reliable play in the defensive zone. D2 has more of an offensive or rushing capability. In addition to playing good defense (the focus is always defense first!), D2 can make quick decisions as to when to jump into the play and has the wheels, eyes, and hands to make something happen on offense.

The distinction is important because responsibilities and mental preparation for D1 and D2 can be quite different. For example, D1 is more the "bear" or the "lion." His mental rehearsal might encompass work on being strong and positionally sound, putting himself between the opponent and the goal he is defending, blocking shots, covering one-on-one and two-on-one situations, and clearing the territory in front of his net. In his mental rehearsal he can see himself being unbeatable, handling the big forwards. When D1 closes in on his opponents, they don't escape him. When he takes opponents to the boards, they're pinned.

On the other hand, D2 is more mobile, like the "jaguar" or the "tiger." D2's mental rehearsal should also include playing good positional defense, but it also features stepping up into the play, rushing the puck, moving to elude a checker, keeping his head up, passing the puck and receiving it, moving in "back door," being strong at the point, having an accurate one-time shot on net, and scoring.

How do you develop skilled defensemen? Pat Quinn, now the coach of the Toronto Maple Leafs, told me, "Good defense starts with learning the fundamentals. First, it's learning to play without the puck. It's learning to play your angles, to position yourself on the inside, to be able to put or move the attack where you want it to come, to play outnumbered, and to protect the goaltender."

Ken Hitchcock, a Stanley Cup–winning coach, concurs. "The single most important lesson that any defender can learn is that he doesn't need to let the puck dictate what will happen. Learn how to invite the puck carrier to do what you want. Soon it will be on his [the defender's] stick."[1]

Quinn also explained how a coach who has a young, inexperienced defensive corps at the NHL or senior level may initially want to adopt a defensive style that protects the defensemen, such as a 1–2–2 trap. In a system like that, the defensemen don't have to bear the brunt of the attack. But, Pat cautioned, "There's a downside to playing in a defensive system all the time . . . This kind of defensive model never builds the offensive side of the player. You may win games 1–0, but the defensemen in this system will always be looking to make the safe play. They'll simply get rid of the puck, dump it out. The result of an overemphasis on this system is that the defensemen can't find the breakout pass and they can't create the rush. They don't learn the transition game and they may never evolve to their offensive potential.

"Until a player has developed to a reasoning stage, to a point where he can read and understand the game," Pat added, "he shouldn't be stuck in a system. Otherwise he will become too dependent on the system; his perceptive, thinking, and offensive skills will be limited. Defensive systems work; they just shouldn't be imposed upon young players too early."

Commenting on youth hockey, Bobby Orr also made the point that it is wrong to impose too much structure and an overemphasis on systems and winning at too early an age. Hockey should be fun for the kids, he says. "Let's teach our kids skills. The Europeans teach their kids the fundamentals, skating, shooting, and passing. We've got to let the kids go. Let them create. They want to learn and have fun. Have them play two-on-two, three-on-three, and four-on-four."[2] Bobby went on to say that if his game had been

---

1 Quoted in *Win with Defense* by Sean Rossiter and Paul Carson (Vancouver: Greystone Books, 1998).
2 Interview broadcast on CKNW Radio (Vancouver), July 24, 2000.

structured when he was a kid, he doubts that he would have ever developed into the player he became.

⚉

At the higher levels, a major challenge confronting the defenseman is how to play against size and speed. Bret Hedican says, "You can't just run at them and knock them down (unless they're off-balance). What's essential is to have good position. My focus is always to be between the opponent and the net."

According to Bret, the best defense against speed is also to maintain good position. "Here, anticipation is very important. Many of the speedy players like Pavel Bure play on the edge, anticipating turnovers. They break to the gap as the puck changes hands. You have to be aware of that, be sure to know where they are and adjust accordingly." Bret's ABCs against players with greater size and speed could be:

A. **Good awareness**
B. **Good position**
C. **Good wheels**

Garry Galley offers the following suggestions, drawn from his 17 years of experience as an NHL blue-liner, on defending against bigger players: "Don't give up space in the neutral zone. Big guys need space to get going, so you can't let them get going. Give them space in the corners. Don't run them. Give them a yard and a half, then take it away. Look for their stick in front of the net. If you can't move the body, take the stick away, and dish out little jabs on the back to distract them and prevent them from getting set."

Garry says the key to playing good defense is to "be in charge." His ABCs are:

A. **Good angles**
B. **Maintain good position**
C. **Know who's on the ice at all times**

"The games when I really play well are the games when I'm alert and in control," Garry says. "I think that when you turn the corner and become a real NHL player, you'll find you know the players in the league, you know the danger areas, and you can control time and space. When you get older, you tend to get smarter. That's when you can take away time and space; [in the process] you spend less time and energy in your zone chasing the man or the puck. Do your work in the neutral zone. Stand up. Turn pucks over, and work hard."

To prepare for a game, Garry likes to relax and run things over in his mind before he goes to the arena. In the dressing room before the game, he'll look at the other team's lineup and think about the opponents' tendencies. "I also find that sharing my thoughts with the younger players helps me to prepare. Usually, I don't know 10 to 15 percent of the players on the other team, so I talk to others in the room about those guys.

"There are also things I say to myself — strategy thoughts about what to do in certain situations; control thoughts like 'Be poised' and 'Be in control in any situation.' [That's important because] younger players feed off the composure of veterans. And I think about creating energy on the ice surface and having confidence with the puck. Consistency is also important. I want to be there and do these things every night. Of course, not every game is an oil painting, but to play good defense you must be in control, consistent, and able to adapt.

"When I'm not feeling in control I take a few deep breaths. I try to stay positive and turn the negatives around."

Garry also repeats something that other players have said: "Many coaches are simply too focused on the negative. You have to let the little things go. Some players don't take criticism very well. I'd say the large majority of players don't know how to use criticism or turn negatives into positives." That's an interesting observation. Turning negatives into positives is an important part of managing the mind. Remember, winners use everything.

After 17 seasons, Garry says he's still learning: "For me it's a learning experience every time I step out onto the ice. Even in the pregame morning skate, I'll skate around and play pucks off the boards and glass to try and get to know the rink, the angles, and the bounces. It may look weird to someone else, but there's always more to know."

⚊○

Chris Pronger, a winner of the Norris (best defenseman) and Hart (most valuable player) trophies, acknowledges the importance of positional play. He says that the great players seem to have a knack for being in the right place at the right time. They can read and react to the puck. If you are going to defend against them, you have to be in the right place — mentally as well as physically.

Chris says that visualization is part of his pregame preparation, but he doesn't tailor his mental rehearsal to the specific team he may be facing that night. Instead, he runs through some positive imagery that he has found prepares him to play against all teams.

I asked Jack McIlhargey about the mental techniques he used to prepare for games during his playing days. Jack said part of his preparation involved using both positive imagery and self-talk to get ready. He would tell himself that he was going to play a good game, then he would imagine himself doing it. "Before every game, I would go over the lineup of the team we were going to play and visualize their players — especially the most dangerous ones. I would see them coming in on me, visualize some of their better moves and see myself playing the body, taking them out of the play, getting the puck, and moving it up — making a good, quick pass."

Once again, Jack said the most important ingredient in playing good defense is to maintain good position. "I always saw myself positioned between the opposing player and our goal." Jack added that another part of preparation is to keep your head in the game while you are sitting on the bench. "Between shifts, on the bench I would watch the way the opposition forwards moved the puck and think about how I would react in each situation. That way my head was in the game and I was ready to play when my turn came up."

Larry Robinson agrees. "Too many guys come off the ice and dwell on what they did out there, especially what didn't go well. I don't think there's enough focusing on the positive aspect of the game. On the bench, it's important to be in the game, watch what the other team is doing, and know what you would do."

When he played, Larry says he didn't really use visualization in a systematic way to prepare for games. Instead, he would rest before games and keep his mind off hockey. "I found that thinking about the game got me too wound up. Especially the games [the Montreal Canadiens played] against the [Quebec] Nordiques. There was so much emotion and pressure to win in those games. I would get too nervous. The most important thing in the game is reaction. I felt I played better when I didn't think too much about the game."

Larry agrees with Luc Robitaille when he says that hockey is different from other sports like football, baseball, and golf in that there are no set plays and most of the game is instinctive. "You've got to react right now. I believe that if a player thinks too much, or if a player has to pause and think about it, he would be late on every play."

Some say, "The worst thing you can do in hockey is think." Obviously, that's a foolish overstatement. A hockey player has to know his job and what to do in every zone on the ice. He has to be able to read a situation, make good decisions, and react. All that involves thinking. Thinking is also the basis of mental preparation, which enables a player to anticipate and react instantly and appropriately. What should be avoided is uncertainty, indecision, and thinking too much. You don't want to be out on the ice trying to decide, "Should I do this or that?"

Thinking is vital to hockey success. How you manage your thinking is up to you. Some players have found it very helpful to run through game situations in their minds immediately before a game in order to sharpen their anticipation and confidence. Others have reported that repeating power thoughts before a game and even between shifts helps them to be more focused and positive. Some players (who feel confident that they know their jobs) find it most beneficial to simply relax before a game. Your style of preparation is a personal decision, but understand that the game's best players are smart players, and playing smart involves thinking.

Adrian Aucoin of the New York Islanders is a power-play expert. One tip he offers to improve in this area is to study the most skilled players when their team has the advantage. "You can learn a great deal by watching other players, like Al MacInnis, quarterback the power play."

Adrian also has some advice about shooting from the point. "When you are playing the point on power plays you want to get the puck to the net but what you want to avoid is shooting into the shin pads of the checking winger. That can create a short-handed goal for the other team.

"There's no one way of imagining yourself shooting from the point. You vary your shooting depending on the situation. For example, if the checker is high and on me quickly, my focus is to shoot to miss his shin pads or his stick by two inches, and in the general direction of the goal. When you have more time and can see the net, then you can pick your spots." Adrian said that he takes a half rather then full swing. "It gives me a quicker release, especially when I'm shooting off a cross-ice pass and I can catch the goalie moving. If the goalie is set and square, I may try and drive it hard, through him."

Toe Blake, legendary coach of the Montreal Canadiens, is alleged to have said, "If you can hear it, it wasn't a good shot." A good affirmation for point shooters is "I put the puck on the net."

I asked Ed Jovanovski for some tips to playing good defense. "The two biggest things for a defenseman are one, position, and, two, patience and poise." Ed's comment brings us back to two basics we discussed at the beginning of the book, namely, right focus and right feeling. Maintaining good position is about focus and making good reads. Patience and poise are feeling states and reflect emotional control. On poise Ed said, "You've got to learn to relax. You just can't play well if you're uptight."

Checking

Checking isn't the same as playing defense. But it is an important aspect of the defensive game. While defensemen essentially protect the area from the opponent's blue line all the way back to their own goal, the checker does much of his defending in the opponent's end and in the neutral zone.

The checker's role is to shut down the other team's scoring line, to stop their aces from moving the puck and going to the goal. A good checker usually plays without the puck more often and for longer than he spends carrying the puck. It's a game of making reads and working hard, doing whatever is necessary to shut the opposition down.

The ABCs of most checkers would include things such as:

A. Skate, skate, skate, go in and come back hard,
   and get where you have to be.
B. Make the right reads.
C. Good positioning, angling, containing,
   taking the body.

Dave "Tiger" Williams was a tenacious checker during his NHL days. But when I asked him about checking, he told me, "The guy you really should talk to is Bob Gainey." So I did.

During his 16 years with the Montreal Canadiens, Bob Gainey set the standard for checking forwards, winning the Frank J. Selke Trophy (best defensive forward) four years in a row. He transformed checking from a trade into a craft and, as a coach and now the general manager of the Dallas Stars, he has helped develop some of the NHL's best checkers.

"From a mental outlook," Bob says, "a checker is a player who finds value in being a difficult opponent." He relies primarily on two tools: skating and intelligence. "A good checker has the ability to get inside his opponent's head. He knows what the opponent will try to do and what he can and can't accomplish." It's important to know when to make a move and when to lay off and let the opponent mess up the play on his own.

Although his value isn't necessarily measured on the score sheet, Bob says that "the really good checker is a two-way player. He's someone who is interested in the puck. Some players aren't — they take it and then they give it right back." Asked for examples of checkers who read the game well and contribute on offense as well as defense, Bob points to Guy Carbonneau (who was a Montreal teammate of Gainey's and then played for him in Dallas) and current Stars right-winger Jere Lehtinen.

Bob says positioning is also an important part of being a proficient checker. "Being effective is understanding and anticipating where the puck will go next, and then getting there. You know, checking is a little like shooting pool — if you're in a good position, there's never any hard shots."

When it comes to checking, Tiger Williams has echoed the same sentiments about positioning as Bret Hedican, Jack McIlhargey, and Pat Quinn: "Always be between your opponent and your net. It's a must to playing good defensive hockey." Tiger went on to say that it's mentally tougher to be a good checker than it is to be a scorer. "A good checker has to talk himself into doing a lousy job, one that's usually unacknowledged, and doing it well." It's often a thankless job. "You can check the top snipers off the score sheet, but when it comes to negotiating next year's salary they look at who scored 30 or 40 goals, and your efforts as a checker are often forgotten."[3]

What sort of mindset does it take to be a successful checker? "Be tenacious," Tiger says, "no matter what the score is. You want the guy you're checking to be thinking to himself, 'Oh, no, not this idiot again. I hope he's not out there again.' When he starts to think, 'Let's wait till next game when I don't have to deal with him,' your job as a checker will be much easier.

"It's during the playoffs that you really find out who the good checkers are, because they have to face the same sniper for five or

---

3 Dave Williams and James Lawton, *Tiger: A Hockey Story* (Vancouver: Douglas & McIntyre, 1984).

six games in a row. It's important for the coach to be committed to you and the matchup, because if he switches you off an assignment the sniper can get the psychological edge."

Brad May, another hard-checking NHL winger, agrees with Tiger about checking and playoff hockey. "There's way more pressure in the playoffs," Brad says. "It's really a challenge to check the best and not only shut them down, but also to beat them." So how does he go about it? "You've got to be smart. You have to be intense and in the moment, but you also have to be in control and balance attacking with an awareness of time and position. Position is key to checking."

The evening before that conversation, I had watched Brad (who was then with the Vancouver Canucks) battling for a playoff berth. Late in a close game, Brad provoked a St. Louis Blues player, who retaliated and got a penalty while Brad skated away. Brad agreed it's hard to walk away from a confrontation, but it's more important in crucial situations to stay under control and play smart hockey.

Brad says checkers have to develop a unique mindset. Once the coach tells you your role, that is all you should think about. "Even when you're sore and beat up, you must gear yourself up and lay it all on the line. I love the intensity. I love the playoffs."

Dave Scatchard of the New York Islanders is a 20-goal scorer who is often asked to play a checking role. According to him, these are the ABCs of checking:

A. **Anticipate. Read the play and be one step ahead of it.**
B. **Good position is key. Put yourself between the opposition player and your goal.**
C. **Communicate with the defense. "Before every face-off, I always make sure we know who's got who. And when necessary we switch."**

Like everyone I asked, Dave stressed the importance of good reads and good position in being an effective checker. "Guys aren't going to be scoring from the corner. Position yourself so they have to go through you to get to the net."

Like defensemen, checking forwards often have to deal with playing against scorers with greater size and speed. "When you're playing against good players, you've got to have good body position," Dave says. "Against big players you have to be in the right place; there's no cheating. You can't reach in and prevent them from getting where they want to go. You have to be there. That's the focus. It's the same when you are playing against speed."

Dave said one of the best examples of consistently good positioning is displayed by Larry Murphy, the veteran defenseman of the Detroit Red Wings. "Larry's not fast," he says. "Most guys in the league are faster, but Larry doesn't get beat — ever — because he has excellent body position."

Good checkers and good penalty killers take pride in shutting down an opponent's scoring line because it's not an easy role to play. A positive attitude toward the challenge makes the job easier. If you are given the role of checker, then choose the assignment. Assume the identity; become the best checker you can be. Imagine yourself as the other player's shadow, or a tiger hunting. Remember what Mark Messier said: "You can create a winning mindset by playing a solid team game. It's important that all the players believe that they contribute and that they make a difference. Whether a guy plays 30 minutes or five minutes, whether he's a scorer or a checker, when everyone believes he makes a difference and plays like he makes a difference, remarkable things can happen. I've seen it."

Chapter 11

Mental Tips on Goaltending

There is no job in professional sport that is the source of greater pressure or stress than being a goaltender in the National Hockey League. Jacques Plante, one of the greatest goalies of all time, once said, "Imagine a job where every time you make a mistake, a red light flashes and 15,000 people stand up and cheer." That's intense pressure.

Many goalies feel that pressure. I have worked with goalies who didn't speak on game days, who vomited before games, and who talked to their goalposts. One NHL goalie's wife told me that her husband got so tense during the season that, in his sleep, he would kick out his legs and flail his arms as if making imaginary saves — and making it very difficult to be in the same bed with him! To survive — and thrive — in that high-pressure environment, a goalie, more than any other player, must master the mental game.

The three things a goalie must learn to manage are his emotions, his focus, and his attitude. Of course, these are the same three qualities that any player must master, but the challenges a goalie faces are unique and more intense. Everyone can make a mistake, but for the goalie the puck (and accountability) stops here!

Tending goal means tending your emotions. Your shift lasts the full 60 minutes, during which you must maintain a razor-sharp edge whenever the opposition has the puck. To survive and excel you have to be able to stay sharp and keenly focused, to be on edge as the puck moves toward your end of the rink, and then be able to release unnecessary tension when the pressure subsides. A key to mastering your emotions and playing winning hockey is to work on the breathing techniques — "release . . . breathe . . . refocus," "turning the wheel," and "being a star," — that I described in Chapter 2.

A goalie has to maintain a sharp focus on the puck and the play for long periods of time. He must know who is on the ice as well as where they are, and he must often fight for clear sight lines to see the puck. He must also be able to tune out such distractions as being jostled or bumped in the crease or allowing a soft goal to bother him. Nothing must affect the goalie's focus or judgment.

Along with breathing and streaming, many of the techniques we described in chapters 3 and 4, such as using positive self-talk, having clear ABCs, being like a cat, and seeing yourself make the plays, can help the goalie to stay on a positive track.

Attitude is what sustains any player through the hockey wars. The key attitude components for goalies are the same as for forwards and defensemen: commitment, confidence, and a positive identity — "I am" and "I can."

I asked several experienced NHL goalies what they thought was the key to their mental game. Glen Hanlon played in the NHL for 13 seasons with the Vancouver Canucks, St. Louis Blues, New York Rangers, and Detroit Red Wings. He saw the game from just about every possible angle — as a starting goalie and a backup, on both winning and losing teams. He learned to perform and excel during the long NHL regular season as well as under the intense pressure that the playoffs entail. After retiring as a player, Glen was an assistant coach with the Canucks for seven years before becoming head coach of the Portland Pirates and winning American Hockey League coach-of-the-year honors.

We worked together throughout his career, and I found Glen a student of the mental game. He incorporated many of the techniques I've described into his preparation and play. I asked Glen what advice he would give to a goalie on the mental game. He started by listing his ABCs:

A. **Preparation**
B. **Position**
C. **Hard work**

By preparation, Glen means physical and mental conditioning. Like Mark Messier and Tiger Williams, Glen believes that physical conditioning is very important to knowing that you're fit and ready. "What some goalies don't realize is that being physically fit builds confidence," Glen says. "Feeling stronger and faster helps you to feel better prepared and to play better. Feeling tired can make you feel slower and more vulnerable. Physical preparation is also about practicing the basics. It's using practice to work on improving your technique for stopping shots, playing the two-on-ones, moving well in the net from side to side, and covering the wraparounds.

"Mental preparation includes mental rehearsal — actually visualizing yourself reacting well in each and every situation. It's imagining yourself performing well in the very same situations you practiced on the ice. And it's seeing and knowing that you can stop the puck in each situation. Then, it's taking that 'knowing' into the game and doing it."

Another part of mental preparation that Glen thinks is vital is managing your emotions. "What helped me was working with my breathing, specifically using my breathing to stay sharp and focused under pressure, and then cool and calm when the pressure is relieved."

By position, Glen means square to the shooter and playing the angles correctly. "Good position has you in the right place to stop the shot," he says. "It can also force the shooter to miss by taking away the net. Hockey is a dynamic game — it's fast and ever-changing. A goalie moving and reacting to the puck can get out of position or 'lost.' A goalie must continually work in practice and in the game to adjust and improve position. Effectiveness and confidence come from knowing where you are and that you are in the right place."

Goalies frequently remind me that a shift for most players lasts less than a minute. In contrast, the goalie is (usually) on the ice for the entire game. It can be a real challenge for a goalkeeper to keep his edge for the full 60 minutes — which take roughly three hours to play. Being in good physical shape makes it easier to meet the intense physical demands of the game, as it is well known that fatigue affects both concentration and attitude. Being in good shape helps you maintain your concentration, your focus, and the belief that "I can."

Glen listed "hard work" as one of his ABCs. He explains that it means doing everything necessary to stay on top of the mental game. "Whenever you notice your attention starting to slip, or when you stop 'mentally attacking' the shooter and start to feel lazy or spacey, or when a negative thought comes to mind, you have to work to refocus and stay positive and sharp. That's hard work, and it's a key to consistent, successful goaltending."

Going into the 1987 Stanley Cup playoffs, Glen wanted some input, something to sharpen the edge. So he gave me a call. I reminded him of what we had worked on over the years: to stay in the moment; to experience one breath at a time, one shot at a time, one period at a time; to see himself making the plays, playing his angles, stopping the shots, and being like a cat. In essence, I reminded him of the basics I've discussed throughout the book: to breathe (right feeling), to focus on the positive (right focus), and to "know" that he was okay (right attitude).

Glen was playing for Detroit, and at first he split the playing time with the team's other goalie, Greg Stefan. Then, after two disappointing losses, his colleague was benched. With the Wings down three games to one in the best-of-seven series — on the brink of elimination — Glen rose to the challenge, shutting out the Leafs by a score of 3–0. Two nights later, he led Detroit to a 4–2 win, then was unbeatable in the seventh and final game of the series, racking up another 3–0 shutout. Glen's play spurred his team into the conference championship against the Edmonton Oilers, who would eventually win the Cup.

The day after that first shutout against Toronto, Glen reflected on his performance: "With about 10 minutes to go in the game, I started to experience some doubt. I recall thinking, 'Something's going to happen; this is too good to last.' Then I noticed what I was thinking, so I took a breath and refocused on the positive. I thought of being like a cat, playing my angles, and being in the moment. After that, I knew I could stop anything." A moment later, he made another big save to preserve the shutout. Glen's ability to stay focused on the positive and be in the moment is the product of preparation and hard work.

John Vanbiesbrouck, a 17-year veteran of the NHL, feels that correct mindset and mental preparation are the keys to consistent high-level performance. Focused hard work in practice was one part of his preparation regimen; the others were appropriate focus on the day of the game and sharp focus throughout the game. According to John, you must use your mind to put yourself in a place where you can excel.

John's ABCs include:

A. **Good position — aggressive, square to the shooter, anticipating.**

B. Focus — keep a puck focus during the entire game, including the commercial breaks. Use the breaks to recharge, rest, and refocus instead of going to the bench to socialize with teammates or space out.

C. Faith and calm — maintain your composure no matter what; don't let anything to upset you.

John's focus and dedication to preparation helped him to excel. But, as he notes, not everyone has the same commitment and work ethic. "I've seen many goalies over the years who didn't make it because they didn't manage the mental game. I remember one very talented young goalie I played with years ago who didn't really know what he needed to do to prepare. It seemed to me that he was always more focused on being a part of what was going on with the guys than he was on really developing his personal strengths. He used to practice hard for 10 minutes, until he thought he could stone everyone, then he'd goof off. The problem is that, when your attention goes in a game and you haven't worked hard in practice to develop the mental discipline and habits to stay focused, then you're simply not able to bring it back. That's what happened to him and it cost him."

I've observed the same thing in junior hockey, where talented young goalies who don't do the preparation and mental work lose their focus during the game — whether because of fatigue, a soft goal, a bump, or even a heckling fan — and are unable to refocus. Without preparation and mental training, many don't develop or realize their potential.

Tony was a promising junior goalie. One night, he was having a good game — he had stopped 42 of 44 shots. His coach described to me what happened next: "There was a faceoff in our end, and I looked over and saw Tony talking back to a fan. I yelled at him, so he stopped. A moment later, the linesman dropped the puck. They won the draw. The puck was passed back to a man at the point, who took a shot and scored.

"I couldn't believe Tony was jawing with a fan," the coach said. "He knows better than that. What was he thinking?"

I was on a road trip with the team, so the coach asked me to have a talk with Tony about his focus. We met the morning after the game. I acknowledged that Tony had played well and made a number of big saves. Then I asked him what happened between him and the fan.

"I don't know why that happened," he said. "This guy was mouthing off and I just started talking back to him. It was foolish."

"Did he say anything particularly offensive?" I asked.

"No. It was the usual nonsense — you know, 'You're a sieve,' 'You're a bum,' that sort of stuff. But for some reason I started talking to him. I know it looks bad when you're doing something like that and then they score."

I reminded Tony of what I had told him before. When "stuff" happens, you have a choice: you either use it, or it uses you. The way to use it is that, if you notice a negative thought, a distraction, or a heckler, you take a breath and send energy out to your hands, feet, and eyes. Be a star. Refocus on your ABCs: position (good angles, square to the shooter), clear focus (see it, then stop it), and be poised for the next shot.

Tony was especially upset because a scout from the University of Michigan was at the game and he had wanted to make a good impression. I suggested that Tony consider the incident a learning experience. "Two years from now, you'll be playing in a college game and the crowd will be noisy and rocking. And then you'll hear some guy in the stands with a loud foghorn voice saying something outrageous about you. And you'll use it to hit the refocus button and make another big save — and smile."

After letting in a questionable goal, the posture of a 15-year-old goalie changed dramatically. Her shoulders slumped and she suddenly looked like she was low on energy and confidence. After the game I told her that her demeanor was important. Regardless of the events in the game she should always project confidence both to her teammates and to the opposition. I shared with her some-thing John Vanbiesbrouck said to me: "Never let anyone know what you're thinking or how you feel." Especially if it isn't positive. I reminded her that she was the boss, and to control her mental TV, release, breathe, and refocus on the positive.

Andy Moog was an NHL netminder for 18 seasons, during which he won 372 regular-season games and three Stanley Cup champi-onships. These days he is an NHL goalie coach who is respected for his experience and focus. "My focus was always first and foremost to stop the puck," Andy says. "I never let the players on the other team get to me. If that happened, I saw it as a win for them; so I didn't let it happen."

Andy says his ABCs boil down to position, or control:

A. Good position, good angles and net awareness,
   square to the shooter, moving under control.
B. Being in control. Nothing distracts me.
C. See it, stop it.

Garth Snow of the New York Islanders is a warrior. He is a very competitive, extroverted player who enjoys the physical aspect of the game. It was Garth who dropped his gloves and skated the length of the ice to get at Marty McSorley after the notorious inci-dent in which McSorley hit Donald Brashear from behind with his stick.

Garth believes that being bumped and pushed around helps to get him into the game and sharpens the edge. However, Garth acknowledges that he has to be careful not to get too pumped or to take the physical stuff too far. That could result in his becoming distracted or overplaying the puck.

The first thing to remember about managing emotions is "know yourself." The second thing is to breathe, release, and refocus. For a goalie, who's on the ice for the full 60 minutes or more, it's essen-tial to stay focused and in control. When I asked Garth for his ABCs, he said he keys on five things:

A. Focus on the puck. See it, stop it.

B. Read the slot (not just the puck). Know who's where on the ice.

C. Be compact and tight. No pucks go through me.

D. Stay square to the puck. That way partial saves and pucks that hit me don't go in.

E. Be patient. Challenge the shooter mentally, but don't commit.

An image I have suggested that goalies use to create the feeling of both challenging and being patient is a tiger hunting — staying in the tall grass, focused, stalking, ready to pounce.

Garth uses mental rehearsal to prepare for games. Specifically, he imagines himself responding to a variety of scoring situations and reacting effectively. Some goalies like to go over the opponent's top shooters, but Garth says he doesn't do that. "I think if I were to mentally highlight a few first-line scorers it could lead to my under-estimating some fourth-line player. And you have to respect and be sharp for everyone in this league."

I talked about goaltending styles with the Leafs Curtis Joseph, one of the NHL's most respected keepers. Curtis describes himself as a more externally rather than technically focused goalie. He says he keeps his head in the game and maintains his focus by constantly being aware of who is on the ice and knowing their plays and ten-dencies. He described it as "instantaneous awareness." He also said he keeps alert by handling the puck, being verbal, and even arguing calls with the referee. He's aware of the importance of maintaining control and knowing when to calm down. Along with taking a breath, something Curtis says he does to calm himself when he realizes he's getting a little over the top is apologize to the referee. With a smile he added, "It takes them by surprise."

Not all the goalies I spoke with over the course of preparing this book have had years of NHL experience. Alfie Michaud was a col-lege all-star who played on an NCAA championship team at the University of Maine and was a finalist for the Hobey Baker Award (college hockey's player of the year). He is one of an intelligent, hard-working breed of young goalies currently playing in the minor leagues. His work ethic, determination, and preparation are impressive for a young player.

Alfie has a clear game-day routine. It begins, as soon as he wakes up, with an early-morning walk, during which he listens to audiotapes that enhance his confidence and emotional control. He is careful to eat well and get plenty of rest. He trains hard, both on and off the ice. He uses positive self-talk to maintain a winning attitude and makes a conscious effort to be positive with teammates. He's a good team player.

Alfie is equally clear about his focus during the game. He described his ABCs as follows:

A. **Be aggressive. Compete. Get out. Challenge the shooter in the troughs. Know that he can't beat me.**
B. **Be patient. Poised. Mentally tough. Don't commit. Play the puck, not the head fake.**
C. **Be compact and tight. Have good position and good angles. Be square to he shooter. Be a wall. Know the puck can't go through me.**
D. **Be quick. Move across quickly and with control.**

Alfie uses a variety of mental skills. He works with his breathing to store and generate energy, to relax, and to stay in his optimal performance zone. He uses positive self-talk — simple thoughts like "Get out. Good angles. Fight through the screen. He can't beat me. Know where the sticks are." To his list we added a few power thoughts: "I'm a star. See it, stop it."

Alfie also uses positive imagery to prepare. For example, he imagines himself with good position and good technique, making all the saves from all the shooters. He said he also uses imagery to increase his confidence by shrinking the net, making it seem smaller in his mind's eye.

Goalies differ in many respects. Just as there are standup goalies and those who play the butterfly style, there are also different personality types among goalies. Many, like Vanbiesbrouck or Moog, are more controlled and they pride themselves on not letting things distract them. I would label them introverted, analytical, and task-oriented. Others, like Billy Smith, Glen Hanlon, Patrick Roy, Curtis Joseph, and Garth Snow are more extroverted, emotional, and confrontational. They believe they get sharper by reacting to the intensity of the game around them, coming out to play the puck, and responding to crease crashers. As I mentioned earlier, the challenge for goalies who react to pressure this way is to assess whether being reactive and getting physical really sharpens their edge or in fact distracts them. If it's the latter, they have to let it go and refocus. Individual differences aside, most goalies who want to excel must master their ABCs. For most, that means:

A. **Good position**
B. **Sharp focus**
C. **Emotional control**

Epilogue to Chapters 9 to 11

As I was wrapping up the writing of this book, I talked with Glen Hanlon. I commented on the many different ways of preparing and focusing that players had. I mentioned how scorers like Pavel Bure and Luc Robitaille didn't really articulate their procedures and apparently did what their instincts told them. Meanwhile others, like Cliff Ronning and Paul Kariya, were quite analytical. Defensemen like Chris Pronger and Garry Galley used visualization, but Larry Robinson preferred not to.

Glen said he thought it was more important for people with defensive responsibilities to analyze and visualize than it was for scorers. "Things are just more structured on the defensive side," he said. "You have to play more in a system. There is a creative element to offense and goal scoring that can't really be structured." This comment echoes what Luc Robitaille said in Chapter 9.

We talked about how superstars like Mark Messier and Patrick Roy were renowned for their preparation. We discussed personality differences and the need for a coach or a sport psychologist to support and communicate with different players in different ways. We talked about how confidence and anxiety can affect performance. Then Glen added a perspective that I agree with, and which I thought was an appropriate conclusion to this section.

"I don't care how good or experienced a player is; if he's doing some mental training and is preparing, thinking, and visualizing, it's only going to make him better."

Chapter 12

Rehab and Recharge

Hockey is a high-speed collision sport played by physically aggressive athletes. As a consequence, injuries are commonplace. Over the years I have counseled a number of players with a wide range of hockey injuries. Most common are injuries to the knees, shoulders, hands and wrists, groin, and neck, as well as concussions and an assortment of bruises and cuts.

The nature of my involvement with hockey injuries is threefold. First, it's to support a player's positive mental attitude about rehabilitation and getting back to playing hockey. Second, it's to show players psychological techniques that can actually facilitate and speed up healing and help to reduce pain. Third, it's to teach them some sport psychology techniques (similar to those I've been describing) that can enhance their on-ice play when they return to the game.

Nobody likes being hurt. However, as I said in Chapter 5, when something happens you have a choice: either you use it or it uses you. If an injured player can accept what has happened, stay positive, be mentally involved in his rehabilitation, and learn some new psychological skills, then ultimately he may use a negative situation to become a better player and a better person.

There's some wisdom to the old saying that an ounce of prevention is worth a pound of cure. Obviously, it's better to prevent injury than to be successful in rehab. Three strategies that I think help hockey players to reduce injuries are:

Be in great shape. Injuries can happen to anybody, but players in excellent shape (in terms of strength, aerobic capacity, and flexibility) are better able to avoid and take a hit.

Keep your head up. The best protection you have is to keep your head up, on a swivel, and with your eyes open so you see what's going on. Awareness enables you to react wisely and quickly. And it's difficult to play smart, safe hockey if you don't play "heads-up."

Be in control. By "control" I mean two things. First of all, control the pace of your play whenever possible. Accidents often happen to people when they are out of control. Being in control also means adopting the attitude of the person who makes things happen rather than the person to whom things happen. Be the boss, not the victim. Take responsibility for playing aggressive, injury-free hockey.

I have observed that when some players experience a minor injury or trauma, a more significant injury will follow. There are several reasons why this happens. Reduced mobility, caused by the injury, makes a player an easier target to hit. Many players also compensate for an injury by changing the way they move, thereby stressing other body parts, which can lead to additional injury.

Another reason why injuries often beget more injuries has to do with the player's mindset. After being "nicked," some players start playing a defensive, "be careful" style of hockey. As I said in Chapter 1, fear causes tension and tension produces fear. Players with an injury who play in a tentative, tight manner sometimes get just what they were worrying about. Playing hurt is painful and anxiety-producing, and for some players it can lead to an unconscious "escape" mentality that also predisposes them to further injury and gets them out of a stressful situation.

$$\Longrightarrow\!\!\bigcirc$$

The increasing speed and size of players, the stick-play, and body contact, make injuries inevitable. A long schedule with lots of travel (teams like the Vancouver Canucks, San Jose Sharks, and Mighty Ducks of Anaheim travel nearly 60,000 miles each season) certainly doesn't help. Given these stressors, I believe the complete player should learn to use a variety of techniques for managing stress, fatigue, injury, and pain. Actually, many of the same techniques we have been discussing to enhance on-ice performance can be adapted to both rehabilitation and between-games recharging.

Three common psychological elements in the rehabilitation of most injuries are relaxation and conscious breathing, positive imagery and self-talk, and a positive attitude. You'll see that these elements will come into play in the examples of hand, groin, back, and knee-injury rehab that follow.

Hand Injuries

As gloves become smaller and more offense-oriented, skates become sharper, and stick-checking becomes more common, so too do hand injuries. A broken hand or a broken or badly cut finger can be a significant injury that makes it difficult, if not impossible, to grip the stick. Further, a stick vibrating from a slash or a hard pass can aggravate the hand. Sometimes, to heal a hand or finger you simply have to take time off from playing (of course, a committed player will continue to work out to maintain his fitness level). That's not always easy for highly motivated athletes to do. Consequently, techniques to accelerate the healing process and help them stay positive and prepare for an effective return are often well received.

In the case of a player with a broken hand or finger, I usually begin by suggesting that the player relax and tune in to his breathing. We focus on the same three breathing qualities of rhythm, inspiration, and direction that I described in Chapter 2. One difference in focus between rehabilitation and performance enhancement is that the primary directional focus for healing is more internal (within the body) than external (what's happening on the ice). That is to say, instead of a player's focusing on his game ABCs, as he would when he is preparing to play, in rehab he is asked to focus on directing his energy to (and through) his injured hand or finger.

Here's how it works. I ask the player to sit back, making himself comfortable with his hand supported. Then he's encouraged to relax and experience a smooth, slow breathing rhythm and to focus on breathing in energy. Next I ask him to direct or imagine a flow of energy through his arm and into the injured hand. With practice he is encouraged to use his imagination to go deep into the site of the injury and to send or stream energy into the spot that is injured. For example, if a player can feel the spot where there is a break in his hand or finger, I ask him to relax, breathe, and stream a soothing, healing energy into and through the injured area and to imagine the bone fusing or knitting.

We know from research findings that as people relax, breathe, and imagine their hands becoming warm, they can actually raise the temperature in their hands. It's not a difficult thing to do. I ran a pain clinic for several years and within just one or two sessions patients were able to "warm their hands" to reduce pain levels. (The technique is especially effective for helping people to manage headaches.) The important point is that you can use your mind — specifically your thinking, your ability to relax, and your imagery — to positively affect your physiology and facilitate healing.

By doing the rehabilitation imagery along with standard physical training therapy and game-related mental rehearsal, a player can return from an injury sooner and be better mentally prepared to play.

An injury is a challenge. Injuries cause anxiety, frustration, and pain. They hurt. They can shatter a player's confidence and plans. They cause separation — being out of the lineup causes most players to feel less a part of the team. The idea of being replaced in the lineup by another player, the uncertainty of whether you will heal, plus the anxiety of how you will play upon returning, all make being injured a very stressful time. These feelings can be moderated by a positive attitude and a constructive approach to rehabilitation — one that includes goal setting, positive self-talk, imagery, and commitment to a good physical therapy program.

As I've said throughout the book, when challenges present themselves it's up to you to use them, rather than let them use you. If you've been injured, use it. Peter Twist, the Canucks' strength and conditioning coach, helps players battle back from injuries all season long. When I asked him how he might advise players to use their injury experience, he said, "I encourage players to capitalize on this time period, both to learn some new mental training techniques and to recondition more intensely then anyone. By doing so, a player can accelerate the healing process and return in better shape than those still in the game. It is a great chance to drive up your conditioning in season and improve specific parts of your game."

Pete Demers, the head trainer for the Los Angeles Kings and president of the NHL trainers' association, said a player's attitude can make a big difference in the effectiveness of his rehab. "Over a quarter of a century I've witnessed tremendous changes in players' thinking about fitness and rehabilitation. We used to have one stationary bike; now we have 15, and they're all being used. Almost everyone wants to work out. Some players show up two hours before practice to work out, and most work out after practice. All the teams have impressive training facilities. There's a widespread, and growing, appreciation that being in great shape means you play better, you have fewer injuries, and you make more money.

"Injuries cannot be completely prevented in a physical sport like hockey, but they can be minimized with training, good equipment, and good nutrition. When injuries do happen, attitude makes an enormous difference in how players rehab. Some players are 100 percent committed to the rehab process. They are highly motivated to get back. They see the value of working hard and have the determination and discipline to focus on their rehabilitation. Not surprisingly, these are the ones who get back sooner.

"I've seen two players with similar injuries. One takes responsibility for his rehabilitation. He's positive, focuses on getting back, works hard physically and mentally, takes care of himself, and does well. Another player with the same injury but doesn't have the same positive attitude feels sorry for himself and expects someone else to do the work for him. Not surprisingly, he doesn't do as well. What you think affects how you train, how you heal, and how you play."

Pete offered one more piece of advice to being a more complete player. He said, "Keep your shifts short — under 45 seconds. Short shifts lead to faster recovery, less fatigue, fewer injuries, and smarter hockey."

Peter Twist also acknowledges the importance of attitude in the rehab process. "A positive attitude enhances the healing process. A negative attitude diminishes the results you accrue from physical training." He suggests players learn to "harness the power of the mind to maximize results and prepare to battle physically and succeed on ice."

Groin Strain

Other common hockey injuries such as groin strain, twisted knees, and sore backs all respond to a similar approach to mental therapy. In each case I usually ask the player to relax and tune in to his breathing, and to draw in energy and then stream it out through the body.

To get a clearer picture of the injury, I often ask players to tune in to the strained or injured area and tell me the size and shape of the discomfort. Is it the size of a dime? a quarter? a silver dollar? an orange? a grapefruit? Is it round? oval? square? rectangular? shaped like a bar or a star? A player with a strained groin may describe the area of discomfort in his groin as shaped like a rectangle, about one inch wide and about three inches long.

Next, I ask players, "If you had to pick a color to describe the discomfort in that rectangle, what color would you choose?" Again, a player with groin strain might respond saying, "It's red . . . a dark red." If I further asked if there were a place where that redness would be most intense, the response might be "Yes, near the top." I might then ask the injured player to go deeper into his breathing and, on the out breath, to send, allow, or imagine a soothing, healing energy flowing into the center of the redness.

The next question I ask is "If you could choose between sending warmth or coolness into the injured area, which temperature would you prefer?" I recall one player with a strained groin replying that he thought warmth would be more beneficial. He went on to say that earlier, when the strain was worse and inflamed, he would have preferred to send coolness into the spot. But the way it felt right then, he preferred to imagine warmth flowing into the strain. Again, I usually encourage the athlete to relax, breathe, and allow the tissues in the area of the redness to relax so that he can send a soothing, warm, healing energy deep into that spot.

In similar cases, I usually suggest that a player spend five to 10 minutes streaming warmth into the soreness, two or three times a day. I also suggest that as he does the gentle stretches prescribed by the trainer, he remember to be conscious of his breathing and that he imagine a feeling of strength and flexibility in his groin.

Sore Lower Back

I usually recommend that a player with a sore lower back lie down on his back with his knees up. This is an ideal position to take strain off the back. I instruct the player to relax and breathe. Again, I ask him to focus his breathing on rhythm, inspiration, and direction. The direction is internal. As before, we begin with streaming

— the five-pointed star. Then we focus on creating a subtle self-induced traction effect by thinking (on the out breath) of sending energy along the spinal column. That means sending energy up through the neck to the top of the head (A), as well as down the spinal column into the tail-bone and then up the knees (B) as illustrated in the diagram.

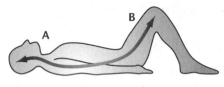

For players with a predisposition to back strain I recommend this breathing and self-induced traction process for a minimum of 10 minutes twice a day throughout the hockey season. Of course, this is in addition to any program of abdominal or core strengthening and stretching recommended by your trainer, physical therapist, or sport physician. A player can treat both back and psyche by relaxing and breathing and doing some mental rehearsal.

Knee Injury

For a player with a knee injury, I also begin by working with breathing — with rhythm, inspiration, and direction. With the player in a comfortable position with his leg supported, I instruct him to focus on streaming energy down through his quadriceps, through his knee to his foot. Then I ask him to relax more deeply and to focus on the specific spot in his knee where he is experiencing most discomfort. One player focused on the inside of his left knee. He described the spot as about the size of a silver dollar. When asked to pick a color that described the pain, he said it was bright red.

I explained to him that, when we are injured, there is often swelling and tension in the area as a result of tissue damage. This swelling and tension serve to protect the area from further injury. I asked him to relax and breathe, to go deep into the injured area and to allow the tissues there to relax. Then I asked him to send a healing, soothing energy deep into the site of the injury. After a few moments of his doing this, I asked him to sense what was going on in that spot and to describe the feeling. He reported that it felt as if something in the knee was twisted. I instructed him to relax and stream energy into the spot and to imagine those tissues untwisting and strengthening.

Along with healing imagery, players are encouraged to do some positive performance imagery (slow-motion mental rehearsal) of themselves skating well, handling the puck, keeping their heads up, passing tape to tape, feeling good, and executing their game ABCs. Being mentally involved in your rehab and using your injury time to strengthen and develop new mental skills can help you to maintain a positive attitude throughout the healing process.

As you can see, with most injuries I advise the player to relax, breathe, and focus on the injured spot. Then I recommend that the player stream a soothing, healing energy into the area. I also recommend that he imagine the antidote to his perceived injury. By that I mean imagine untwisting whatever feels twisted, strengthening what has been stretched, or fusing what has been fractured. If you feel an inflammation, you may want to cool it. If it's more of a chronic injury, or something you've had for a while, you may want to send warmth into the spot. It can help to visualize coolness and warmth as colors. Blue and green are cooling, healing colors. Soft reds and golds are warming, healing colors.

As I have said, these suggestions are meant to accompany and supplement physical treatment and physical therapeutic exercises. Here are some of the keys to the psychology of rehabilitation:

1. Being positive and taking response-ability for effecting change.
2. Doing the appropriate physical rehab.
3. Releasing tension (dis-ease) and sending a soothing, healing energy to and through the area.
4. As you begin to make progress, it's important to imagine yourself playing again — playing well and with confidence. First, imagine skating with ease and in slow motion, and then, gradually, with jump and speed if it's a leg injury. Imagine handling the puck and then shooting well and pain-free if it's

a wrist injury. The idea is to feel yourself doing the things you do well and to visualize yourself doing them — first in slow motion, then at game speed.

5. It is also important to talk positively to yourself throughout your rehabilitation period. Create and train with affirmations (see Chapter 3). A few good, healing affirmations are "One step at a time," "Every day I'm getting stronger and better," and "Smoother, faster, stronger." Make the injury and your time away from the ice a period when you are going to improve your mental skills so that you return to the game mentally stronger and a more complete player.

Concussions

There is both a growing awareness of and a concern about concussions in hockey. Many players play down a blow to the head — "It's just a dinger" — and try to return to the ice as soon as possible. The problem is that, if a player returns too soon after a concussion, he is three times more likely to suffer a second concussion. The reason is that concussions can temporarily reduce on-ice awareness and slow reaction speed. Many players have said that when they are well they have a sort of sixth sense that tells them when someone is closing in and they are about to be hit. This enables them to react and avoid the hit. It's as if this sixth sense provides a protective umbrella around the player. After a concussion, players report that this sensing ability is diminished or gone. They are just not as aware of someone about to hit them, they are slower to react, and they are more vulnerable to a second head shot.

It's also important to understand that there are cumulative effects of concussion, and a second concussion is likely to be more serious then the first. There is a phenomenon as well called "second impact syndrome," which means that the effects of a second head trauma occurring shortly after the first can be very serious. In part, that's because the body's natural ability to minimize brain swelling following a concussion is reduced for a time after the first concussion. As a result the effects of a second concussion occurring soon after the first can lead to irreversible swelling, permanent damage, and even death. This is especially the case in younger athletes. Again, in general, the effects of repeated concussions are cumulative.

Most of the professional and junior hockey teams I've been involved with over the past couple of years are doing some simple psychological testing of their players to establish a "mental baseline." This is a good idea. Following a concussion, an injured player can now be retested, and the results of his post-concussion scores can be compared with his pretest scores. Significant drop-offs in performance on memory, orientation, and awareness tests indicate reduced brain functioning and can help to determine if and when a player should return.

But the test should not be the sole determinant of whether a player is ready for action. I had a telephone call from an NHL player who had experienced a grade three concussion, the most serious level. It is characterized by a loss of consciousness following the trauma. It had been a week since his concussion, and he told me that his scores on the memory and orientation scores were good and that the training staff had said he should be ready to go back in a couple of days. When I asked him how he actually felt, he reported that he was still having headaches when he exercised and that he felt a kind of "wobbliness" at times. He said that, even though his test results were okay, his thinking wasn't as clear as before. I told him that when it came to managing his recovery, he was the boss. I advised him not to return to the game until he was symptom-free for at least one week.

There's a macho code in hockey that expects players to "suck it up," get right back on the ice, be a tough guy, and not let their teammates down. It applies to most injuries, and even more so in those instances where there is no outward sign of an injury. The problem is that players tend to minimize concussions. "It's nothing, I just got my bell rung. I'm not bleeding, there's no significant pain, so I'll play." And they do. However, the functional life consequences of a permanent brain injury are far more significant than the consequences of permanent knee damage.

In a brochure on concussions prepared by the Canadian Hockey Association, Nick Kypreos — whose NHL career was shortened by multiple concussions — recalled his last one, which he suffered in a fight during an exhibition game:

> I lost my helmet and my head hit the ice. It's like a dream you can't remember. Within one hour everything started to come back into focus. I was being asked how I was feeling and if I could go back and finish the game." Players should not be asked that question. "They're too emotional to answer. You just want everyone to forget it ever happened . . . to keep playing hockey. Since I was seven years old I've been told to 'shake it off,' 'dust off the cobwebs,' 'suck it up and you'll be fine' . . . The days of sniffing smelling salts are over. You can see a knee or shoulder injury but you can't see a head injury, so there is always a question of 'How hurt is he?' Only a doctor should decide when the player should return to the game.[1]

Here is a guideline for players, coaches, trainers, and parents on concussion management in amateur sport.

Signs and Symptoms of Concussion

- Any period of loss of consciousness (paralytic coma, unresponsiveness to arousal)
- Vacant stare (befuddled facial expression)
- Delayed verbal and motor responses (slow to answer questions or follow instructions)
- Confusion and inability to focus attention (easily distracted and unable to follow through with normal activities)
- Disorientation (walking in the wrong direction; unaware of time, date, and place)
- Slurred or incoherent speech (making disjointed or incomprehensible statements)

---

1 Quoted in *Concussion Awareness* (brochure prepared by the Canadian Hockey Association, 1999). Reprinted by permission.

- Gross observable incoordination (stumbling, inability to walk tandem/in a straight line)
- Emotions inappropriate and/or out of proportion to circumstances (distraught, laughing, or crying for no apparent reason)
- Memory deficits (exhibited by the athlete repeatedly asking the same question that has already been answered, or inability to memorize or recall three of three words or three of three objects in five minutes)
- Complaints of headaches, dizziness, seeing stars or colors, ringing in the ears, nausea/vomiting, impaired vision, sensitivity to light[2]

Mental Status Testing

Orientation:

- Time, place, person, and situation/circumstances of injury

Concentration:

- Digits backward (i.e., 3–1–7, 4–6–8–2, 5–3–0–7–4); months of the year in reverse order

Memory:

- Names of teams in previous contest
- Recall three words and three objects at zero and five minutes (e.g., white rabbit, red apple, blue car)
- Recent newsworthy events
- Details of the contest (plays, moves, strategies, etc.)

Additional Symptoms:

If there is any appearance of headaches, dizziness, nausea, unsteadiness, blurred or double vision, sensitivity to light, and/or inappropriate emotions, get immediate help from a medical professional.

---

2 The information in *Concussion Management in Amateur Sport* was prepared by the British Columbia Brain Injury Association and the British Columbia Ministry of Children and Families and is endorsed by the British Columbia Pediatric Society and the Sport Medicine Council of British Columbia. I was a member of the board of directors of the British Columbia Brain Injury Association while these recommendations were being drawn up. I was also a founder of the Pacific Coast Brain Injury Conference Forum(s) on Concussion in Sport.
Reprinted by permission.

Recommended Physical Evaluation:

(for grade one concussion only):

- 40-yard sprint, five push-ups, five sit-ups, five knee bends

Grades of Concussion

Grade One

- No loss of consciousness
- Transient confusion (inattention, inability to maintain a coherent stream of thought and carry out goal-directed movements. An athlete commonly refers to getting a "ding" or having his "bell rung." He may attempt to keep on playing.)
- Concussion symptoms and mental status abnormalities on examination lasting less than 15 minutes

Grade Two

- No loss of consciousness
- Transient confusion (inattention, inability to maintain a coherent stream of thought and carry out goal-directed movements. An athlete commonly refers to getting a "ding" or having his "bell rung." He may attempt to keep on playing.)
- Concussion symptoms and mental status abnormalities on examination lasting more than 15 minutes

Grade Three

- Any loss of consciousness, whether brief (seconds) or prolonged (minutes)

Management Recommendations

Grade One

- Remove the player from the contest.
- Examine immediately and at five-minute intervals for the development of mental status abnormalities or post-concussion symptoms — at rest and with exertion.
- May return to contest after 48 hours if mental status abnormalities or post-concussive symptoms have cleared.

Grade Two
- Remove the player from the contest and disallow from returning that day.
- Examine on-site frequently for signs of evolving mental status abnormalities.
- A medical professional should re-examine the athlete the same day.
- A physician should perform a neurological examination to clear the athlete for return to play after one full symptom-free week, at rest and with exertion.

Grade Three
- Transport the athlete from the field to the nearest emergency department by ambulance if still unconscious or if worrisome signs such as neck pain are detected with cervical spine immobilization.
- A thorough neurological evaluation should be performed emergently, including appropriate neuro-imaging procedures when indicated.

My own personal feeling is that, if there are any ongoing symptoms such as confusion, inability to focus attention, slurred speech, emotional lability (mood swings), memory deficits, or being slow to answer questions or follow instructions, then the player simply should not play. I believe that, following a concussion, a player should consult with a sport medicine physician and be completely symptom-free (both during and following intense physical exercise) for a minimum of a week before he returns to the game.

When I discussed concussions with Pete Demers, the NHL's most senior trainer, he said, "I think psychological help is useful in assisting players who are healing from injuries. This is especially true when dealing with a concussion. Following a concussion, many players are anxious and their self-esteem is low. Some players fear they will never be right again. Frequent neurological evaluations are beneficial to find out what is going on, but one-on-one support is extremely beneficial in reassuring the athlete, helping him deal with the inevitable fear and frustration that go with a head injury, and, when appropriate, helping him to return to the game."

Recharging

I was talking to a first-line junior player about motivation. "How many shifts do you get a game?" I asked.

"About 20, maybe 25," he said.

"How many shifts usually decide the outcome of the game?" I asked.

"I guess two or three," he replied.

"Well, to be successful, you have to play as if each shift is a game-breaker. And you have to play that way every night."

Hockey is a physically and mentally demanding game. You are expected to give 100 percent on the ice. When you step off the ice, I believe you should have a way to recharge and reload. I think it's advisable to have techniques that you can use to recharge as part of your pregame preparation or for postgame recovery.

I often make tapes for my clients. You may wish to edit this script to suit your patterns and preferences, then make a tape of it so you have your own relax-recharge tape.

Sit or lie back. Turn off the TV or radio. Make yourself comfortable. Allow the weight of your body to be supported by whatever you are resting on.

Now bring your attention to your breathing. First, pay attention to your breathing rhythm. By that I mean give yourself time for the breath to come in . . . and give yourself time for the breath to go out. The breath is like waves in the ocean, and the waves never rush. Take time as you breathe to feel the in wave, or the in breath, come in . . . and feel the out wave and the out breath go out. You deserve your time.

Breathe smoothly and easily and imagine energy flowing through your shoulders and arms, into your hands. (Repeat.)

Breathe easily and allow energy to flow down through your pelvis and legs, into your feet. (Repeat.)

Breathe easy and allow energy to flow up the spinal column, up into your head. (Repeat.)

Breathe easy and allow energy to flow out to your hands, feet, and head, like a five-pointed star. (Repeat.)

Breathe easily and think of energy flowing to you and through you.

Understand that you have a personal connection to an unlimited supply of energy. Wherever you are, with each breath, you can tap that energy supply. Breathe easily. Feel yourself drawing in energy and sending it out through you.

If any part of your body feels tense, sore, or tired, think of breathing in energy and sending a soothing, relaxing, recharging energy into that part of your body. Think of breathing in new energy, and breathing out used energy.

Remember, your breath is like waves in the ocean, and over time the waves can wash away tension, tiredness, and fatigue.

With each in breath, think of breathing in new energy. On the out breath, release tension, tiredness, and fatigue.

Allow energy to flow to you and through you.

Allow waves of energy to wash through you.

For pure relaxation, remember the recharging imagery we discussed in Chapter 4 and add the image of being in a relaxing/recharging place to your breathing, streaming process. Select an imaginary setting that would be a comfortable, safe, healthy, recharging space where you could tap an abundance of good-quality energy and where there would be no distractions. The examples I mentioned in Chapter 4 were a beach with the waves rolling in, a mountaintop with clean, fresh air, the refreshing quiet of a cabin in the woods, and the comfort and security of your own room.

You can create an imaginary space of your own. One NHL player told me how he loved horses. When he was at home, to relax, he would go for a ride the afternoon of a game. On the road, he would relax in his hotel room and imagine himself riding in the country-side. The idea again is that on a plane or a bus, or in a hotel far from home, you can simply close your eyes, imagine a recharging place, slip into your breathing, and stream energy through your body and recharge. If you have a big game or an early flight and can't get to sleep, this technique will give you a quality relax/recharge program to tune in to. Trying unsuccessfully or forcing yourself to get to sleep only causes more tension. With this technique, even if you don't sleep, you will recharge — and that awareness reduces the pressure to get to sleep, which in turn makes it easier to sleep.

Before a game, if you are feeling rested and you then want to do some game-related imagery, imagine playing in slow motion — skating well, feeling strong and fast, being smooth, having great hands, great wheels, and clear eyes, and making all the moves.

Lifestyle

When I address any group of high-performance athletes I remind them of one thing that helps cultivate their continuous develop-ment and success: lifestyle — quite simply, the way we live from day to day. That includes our diet, exercise, rest and recreation, rela-tionships, and attitude. As in any group, there are vast lifestyle differences among hockey players. The following are some general comments that apply to most players in each of five areas.

Diet

When I worked for the Los Angeles Rams of the NFL, I remember cringing at the fast food–heavy diet of some of the players — for instance, Coca-Cola and doughnuts for breakfast. The players' parking lot was filled with high-priced luxury and sports cars, so I told some of the players, "You wouldn't put that junk food in your car and expect it to perform well. Why do you put it in a high-per-formance energy system like your own body?"

There are many theories and fads about diet, and there are also marked individual differences in metabolism, experience, and preference. While younger players often feel they can eat anything (and they do) without its affecting them, more mature players tend to have developed an awareness about how the foods they eat affect their performance. In general, most experts recommend a diet rich in complex carbohydrates, high in fiber, and low in fat, with a moderate amount of protein. Plenty of fluids are also advised.

For pregame meals, eat something that is easy to digest. Again, if you're like most players, you'll probably be loading up on complex carbs. But experiment intelligently and find out what works for you. Think about the foods you're used to and try to recall what has nurtured good performances in the past. If you keep a performance journal, it's a great idea to make notes about the effect of what you eat on the way you play.

Exercise

Most hockey players get plenty of exercise during the season, and players are increasingly working out and building strength and fitness all year long. Physical training is a great way to prove the old saying that what you put in (to your training) is what you get out (in performance and power).

Work hard. But remember, you are not a machine. Whenever you can, balance activity and rest. Take a month off during the off-season and find ways to cross-train. And remember what has been said earlier: fitness and strength build confidence and aid concentration.

Rest and recreation

Rest is essential to maintaining a balance between work and activity on the one hand and recharging and passivity on the other. Rest is vital, and it should be quality rest. You can improve the quality of your rest by developing some relaxation or meditation techniques like those presented earlier in this chapter and in Chapter 2. Sleep is also very important. Just as you schedule training, get sufficient rest and meet your sleep needs.

Recreation means "re-creation." The most popular recreational "activity" in North America is watching television. This is neither renewing nor recharging. Balance activity with passivity, action with rest, habit with spontaneity, and do things that are fun. There can be many distractions around the game of hockey, especially at the higher levels. Make time for yourself to rest and recharge free of distraction and energy-draining activities. Develop a good R&R program.

Marty was a young player who had to play an intense, high-energy game to be effective. During his first call-up to the NHL he got sidetracked by the night life. When he was sent back down to the minors he acknowledged that he hadn't developed any sense of balance. It was go, go, go on the ice and go, go, go at parties and clubs afterward. His preparation was inadequate, his play became inconsistent and flat, and he was sent to the minor leagues. Fortunately for Marty, he learned from his experience and recommitted himself to the game. Part of that meant learning how to rest and recreate in a way that helped him to be charged and ready to play hard on the ice, on every shift.

Relationships

We are social animals. Whether you are introverted or extroverted, people- or task-oriented, the relationships you form with others are an important part of your life. Career hockey players who invest a great deal of energy in their game usually rely on and benefit from nurturing, supportive off-ice relationships with their wives, girl-friends, parents, and friends. If you are fortunate enough to have one or more such relationships with someone who supports you, your needs, your moods, and your anxieties during the season, remember that the off-season is time to pay them back and it's your turn to spend time and energy nurturing and supporting them.

I remember phoning one NHL player during the off-season while he was immersed in family responsibilities. When he answered the phone it was clear that he had his hands full. He was bathing his baby daughter and trying to persuade his four-year-old son not to do something. It wasn't easy, and he knew it. He summed up his appreciation of the situation by laughing and saying, "Where's hockey practice when I need it?"

Hockey players both young and old have had their careers nurtured by a woman in their lives — a mother, wife, or girlfriend. I remember the wife of an NHL tough guy telling me that the player demanded that she have his pregame meal prepared for him at exactly one o'clock. If his meal was late he would get very upset and complain loudly. She tried her best to accommodate him; however, she was a busy housewife and mother with many other things to do, and occasionally, inevitably, his pregame lunch would run late. When I asked her how she handled that, she smiled and said, "Real simple: I just turned the clock in the kitchen back to twelve-thirty."

Create supportive relationships that help you relax, prepare, and play the game. And maintain them. Appreciate what others do for you, acknowledge their love and support. And remember, it's payback time in the off-season.

Attitude

Again, attitude is a matter of choice and it's a key component to a healthy lifestyle. Choose to be positive. We talked about a winning hockey attitude (commitment, confidence, and identity) in Chapter 5. Three elements of attitude that I would like to remind you to bring to your daily life are courage, gratitude, and love.

By courage, I mean that you should have the heart to set life goals that challenge you — and the heart to work toward meeting these goals. By gratitude, I mean appreciate what you have, and don't dwell on what's missing. Many players know people who are sick, disabled, or far less fortunate than they are. Don't sweat the small stuff. Every day, be grateful for your health and energy and the opportunity you have to enjoy playing a game you love. By love, I mean accept and respect people and opportunities in your life. Be kind and positive to the people you work with and to those who support you. And follow the Golden Rule: Do unto others as you would have them do unto you.

HOMEWORK: ⫸

There are two homework assignments for Chapter 12.

Assignment 1 ⫸

Even if you are injury-free, find a tense, sore, or tired spot or muscle group and practice relaxing, breathing, and streaming energy to and through that area. Try to get a picture of the size, shape, and color of the area. Think about sending heat or coolness to the affected area.

Assignment 2 ⫸

Create or select a recharging image of a power place where you can go to recharge. Then, every day for a week, spend 15 minutes practicing bringing that image to mind and breathing, streaming, feeling like a star, drawing energy to yourself, and letting it flow through you.

Chapter 13

Growing Talent and Fostering Hockey Values

Over the course of the first 12 chapters I've discussed some of the psychological elements and mental training techniques to help an athlete become a more complete hockey player. A theme that has come up again and again is the importance of managing emotions, maintaining composure, and using adversity in a positive way to refocus and become more effective. The complete player is one who can exercise control in the face of challenge and adversity.

The past couple of years there have been marked by a number of violent incidents in the game of hockey. One particularly shocking incident occurred in July 2000, during a 10-year-old boys' practice game in Reading, Massachusetts. Two of the players' fathers got into an altercation that resulted in one father beating the other to death in the parking lot adjacent to the arena while the youngsters looked on. At the pro level, in the final moments of an NHL game between Boston and Vancouver on February 21, 2000, the Bruins' Marty McSorley skated up behind Donald Brashear of the Canucks and hit him over the head with his stick. Brashear experienced a concussion and seizure. It was a dangerous, violent act committed by a player who was frustrated and angry and lost control.

These incidents have attracted a great deal of media attention. They also initiated much discussion about violence and values surrounding the game of hockey. They are examples of what can happen when self-control is not exercised.

Hockey is a wonderful sport. It's fast, exciting, physical, creative, and tough. Teamwork is at the heart of the game. Of course the objective is to win, but win at what price? And where is it most appropriate to put the emphasis at the developmental levels? Should young players be encouraged to develop sound fundamentals and laudable core values? Or should they be taught to do whatever it takes to win, to suck it up and tolerate undisciplined violence?

I'm not interested in taking an editorial stand as to whether or not there should be fighting in the NHL. The NHL is sport, entertainment, and business. We should be absolutely clear, however, that modeling is a very powerful form of learning. Children imitate their elders, especially the sport stars and hockey players they idolize. And, there is a significant trickle-down effect of violence in pro sport influencing the way kids play the game.

What I find disturbing is the violence that occurs at the younger, developmental levels. I believe it is the result of a disproportional emphasis on winning as well as a lack of reinforcement of the values of respect and discipline.

A bantam elite team (14- and 15-year-olds) I worked with finished league play in first place with a very good record. One of the things the team prided themselves on was their on-ice focus and discipline. The team had drawn less than half as many penalty minutes as any other team in their league. In the first round of their league playoffs, a best-of-three series, they won the first game 4–1, and were winning the second handily by a score of 5–1. With about five minutes left to play, an opposition player picked a fight with one of our team's smallest players — a young man who had a total of four penalty minutes the entire season. The bigger player knocked off the smaller player's helmet and proceeded to beat him up. The smaller player's nose was badly broken and required surgery. He missed the next month of hockey, including the rest of the league playoffs and the provincial championships.

In the playoff series that followed there was more nonsense. With the score tied in the third period of game two, an opposing player ran the goalie, who was on his knees covering a shot. The forward kneed the goalie in the head, knocking him unconscious and loosening several of his teeth. These two examples represent different expressions of violence. The first case is an example of violence as a release of frustration and anger. A player was frustrated that his team was losing and about to be eliminated so he took his frustration and anger out on his opponent. The second is an example of doing whatever you have to do to win — in this case, take the goalie out of the game.

I don't see a place for either form of violence in bantam hockey. As one parent said to me, "I support my son playing hockey. That doesn't mean I give some bully permission to beat his brains out." These are kids playing hockey. At this developmental level, hockey should be about teaching children hockey skills, quality life values such as teamwork, discipline, and respect, and about having fun.

When I spoke with Bobby Orr on the subject of youth hockey, he said he was concerned that many youngsters are moving away from sports because it's simply not fun. "There's way too much of an emphasis on winning. There's too much violence, and too much playing the system. It's just not fun." Orr went on to say that one of the sad consequences of the kids leaving hockey (and other sports) is that they don't learn many of the values that the game can teach, like teamwork, discipline, and respect for others.

A few years ago I sat on a panel that discussed the importance of keeping children in sport, because children in sport are more apt to stay in school. When children leave the game they lose an opportunity to learn some of the positive values that the game can teach them. They become more vulnerable to some of the negative social forces, and that lost opportunity is a tragedy.

For the past seven years I have worked with teams in junior hockey. One phenomenon I have witnessed is that some teams send out players to "attack and hack" the opposing scorers. In consecutive years, I have seen top scorers on teams I've been involved with being slashed and chopped with two-handers. In one case a leading scorer was slashed and his hand broken in the first game of a playoff series. This doesn't seem remarkable until you consider that the same player had been knocked out of the playoffs by the same team the year before with a violent cross-check. Coaches around the junior leagues tell similar stories about violence repeatedly being directed against many of the league's star players. While this undoubtedly develops toughness among those that survive, it raises questions as to whether this is the best direction for the game, and whether this is the best way to develop talent.

I spoke at a junior hockey "showcase" to about a hundred 14- to 16-year-old players and their parents. A comment I heard several times from parents who approached me after my talk was "My son is a good player, but I don't know if he's mean enough to play junior hockey." I find that perception disturbing. If these parents said that their son wasn't tough enough, I'd say, "Toughness is part of the game. But *mean* isn't."

Sadly, in my experience there are many players, coaches, and parents in amateur hockey (bantam, midget, junior, and high school) who *do* think the game is to win at any price, including violence. They simply have little to no respect for the well-being of the players on the other team. And their behavior reflects that value.

Again, I want to be clear. By violence I am not referring to crushing body-checks. Hockey is a high-speed, collision sport and the big hit is an exciting and integral part of the game. Rather, I am talking about stick-work like slashing and chopping opponents, high elbows, vicious cross-checks, blatantly late hits, kneeing, and premeditated fighting.

Who is responsible for violence in hockey? I think the answer is everyone involved — players, coaches, parents, league officials (including referees), and spectators. All have to exercise their response-ability to effect change. As players and coaches are the primary audience of this book, I'd like to focus on what they might do.

Players can be more response-able and exercise more control. As I've said throughout this book, you're the boss. You control the switch. You can always change channels.

I tell the players on all the teams I'm involved with that they have a choice. "If someone or something pisses you off, use it in a positive way to refocus and to make yourself more effective. Or park it. The ultimate putdown is to stuff the puck in the other team's goal. And, if you don't want to fight or retaliate (and end up in the penalty box), you can always skate away." As I said in Chapter 6, mental toughness is your ability to stay focused (and have a positive impact on the game), no matter what.

I coach players to have emotional control and discipline by taking a breath, changing the channel, and parking an angry thought. Here's what Dave Scatchard of the New York Islanders had to say about the work we did on control and focus: "The breathing work has really been helpful. There were times when I was starting to snap, like after I had been tripped or speared, or when someone did something dirty to me and I couldn't retaliate. I wanted to go crazy but I was able to use the breathing to calm me down and help me to get my focus back."

In Chapter 8 I related a story about Mark, a junior defenseman who snapped — he lost control and cost his team a game. Mark had a problem controlling his impulses and his temper. After the incident, Mark felt bad that he had let the team down. It was clear he needed some coaching in managing his emotions. I reviewed the release, breathe, refocus process with Mark and encouraged him to use it on the ice. If he came off the ice angry, I showed him a process and gave him some things to say to himself to cool down. In addition, when he was penalized, the coach was advised to send another player (preferably a team leader) over to the penalty box to remind Mark to calm down and be cool when he stepped back onto the ice.

In situations where penalties can have severe consequences, such as in overtime, or during the playoffs or the Olympics, players can usually be relied upon to exercise considerably more self-control and restraint than in routine play. Far fewer players take ill-advised penalties, and the hockey is better.

Of course, that's not always the case. Tie Domi momentarily lost control in the 2001 playoffs and knocked the New Jersey Devils' Scott Niedermayer unconscious with a blind-sided elbow to the head. After the incident, Tie, a highly motivated team player, was sad and embarrassed by his actions and the suspension that disqualified him from further participation in the playoffs.

Before to the playoffs I asked Tie how he manages to play an aggressive, physical game and yet maintain control. He said, "You've got to have control. When things start to get away from you, you've got to take a few deep breaths and then refocus on all the little things you've got to do." It's clear that even for an experienced player in a big game, that can sometimes be easier said then done.

When asked about the Domi incident, Chris Pronger, the St. Louis Blues all-star defenseman, commented, "Ninety-nine percent of the time you might have a thought about doing something like that — thinking 'I'm going to get that prick' — but then something in your head clicks on and stops you from doing it. In this case it didn't click on." Chris added, "It's hard to be sympathetic to someone who does something like that."[1]

Most players can reduce violence by exercising greater control when they choose to do so, and when it would hurt their team to be penalized. The complete player is one who can exercise control in the face of challenge and adversity. Having said that, more emphasis can and should be placed on teaching players emotional control skills. I believe it would make for better hockey.

Coaches are response-able and can exercise more control to

---

1 Interviewed on The Team Radio Network, May 8, 2001.

shape a team's values and behavior. On one occasion I was sitting in the stands behind the bench of a visiting junior team. They were losing a hard-fought game, 5–3. As the end of the game neared, the play became more physical, and some of the visiting players grew agitated and verbal, yelling abuse at players on the ice and on the bench. I could sense a fight brewing. What was disappointing was that the visiting coach made no effort to control the behavior of the players on his bench. In fact, he sent them onto the ice and a fight ensued. It was unnecessary. It added nothing to the game. It was nothing more than a release of anger. The situation could have been managed differently, but the coach's handling of it clearly reflected his own values and lack of control.

Coaches have tremendous power in hockey. If you want approval and ice time you had better please the coach. The coach decides who will play and how much ice a player will get. If players don't conform to the team's plan and values, the coach can simply choose not to play them. And if the coach demands discipline and tough, hard, controlled play, that is what he will get.

Ron Wilson, the coach of the Washington Capitals, relates a story from his playing days about the late Bob Johnson. "If you did something wrong, Johnson wouldn't yell at you, he just didn't play you. You found yourself sitting. You might miss a couple of shifts or even a period. After a couple of periods of sitting, you were very motivated to change your ways, and even to say, 'Coach, I don't know what I did, but I promise I'll never do it again!'"

A coach can have even greater influence in youth hockey where children are more impressionable and dependent. I believe coaches can be more response-able in managing their power and influence. When a coach sends a couple of 15-year-old goons out onto the ice to start a fight in the dying minutes of a hockey game that his team is losing, that coach should be held accountable and penalized.

It bears pointing out that many developmental coaches value a tough but clean brand of hockey. And they give their time and energy because they care about the kids and the game. One example is Bob's Program. Bob Tunstead is a successful businessman who played minor professional hockey in the United States and in Europe who for the past 15 years has been coaching young hockey players. For several years he has been coach of a bantam AAA team in Kelowna, British Columbia. The boys on Bob's team are 14- and 15-year-olds. We've worked together for the past four seasons.

The squad he selected last year was not blessed with an over-abundance of talent. At the start of the season, several of the other teams in the bantam elite league had a number of their players listed as prospects by various major junior clubs in the Western Hockey League. Bob's team had none. When the season was over, not only was Kelowna's record an outstanding an 18–2 but the club's penalty-minutes total was less than half the league average.

I asked Bob how he managed to create a winning team and help his young charges play a hard, tough, clean, high-quality hockey game. He said he sets a tone at the start of the season by establishing a system of values — detailing how the players are expected to act on and off the ice. To ensure the players will buy into his program, Bob sits down with each player to explore his individual and team goals. Some want to play junior hockey in the Western or British Columbia hockey leagues; others want to get a university hockey scholarship or win a provincial championship; still others simply hope to develop their hockey skills. Bob then makes it clear what he expects from them in terms of behavior, including hard work, team play, punctuality, and no swearing. He tells the boys, "I'll build a foundation that will help you achieve your goals, if you commit to following the program." It is presented as a win/win opportunity and the players agree.

Scotty Bowman has said a team must have an identity. When I asked Bob's bantam AAA team what their identity was, the boys responded by describing themselves as "hard working [for three periods], disciplined, intelligent, well-prepared, and winners." Bob pushes the boys to work hard on and off the ice. They are put through a challenging regimen of conditioning, power-skating drills, and fast-moving practices. Drills are designed to develop skills and to be fun.

He also asks the players to keep a hockey journal, in which they are to write down their goals, the skills they wish to improve, and how they prepare for and perform in each game. He encourages them to be honest and to review and compare their approach to games in which they feel confident and play well with those days when they don't play as well. He also asks them to record what they were doing in practice to improve their skills, whether it's lengthening their skating stride, making more accurate passes, or having more discipline about executing the system in the defensive zone. Bob asks his players to mentally rehearse how they would perform in games at both ends of the ice. They review their ABCs, use positive self-talk, and are expected to communicate positively with their teammates.

Before games, he suggests players relax, stretch, ride the stationary bike, and visualize themselves working on a couple of aspects of their game. Once a month, Bob reviews their journals and asks each player to rate his play. Then he evaluates the player's self-assessment and discusses it with him. "At first, some kids experienced some denial," Bob observes. "They might pick someone on the team who wasn't playing well and say, 'Compared to him, I think I'm doing great.'" Bob would take the focus off the other players. "Compared to *you*," he would ask them, "what can you do to be better?"

Bob looks at the way developmental hockey programs are run in North America and offers this observation: "Coaches simply have to take more responsibility for how the game should be played and relay that message to their players."

Bob acknowledges that sport psychology has made a valuable contribution to his teams. "I think it is an important part of the skill package. It can help players to control their emotions. Breathing can help settle them down in intense situations, and that reduces penalties. It can help them to stay positively focused and to provide support from the bench. Too many players experience too many negative thoughts prior to and during the game. Sport psychology can also help them to maintain the right focus. It can help them to visualize and prepare. When players prepare properly, they're less nervous. They come to the rink more confident and focused on playing to the best of their ability."

Then Bob shifted gears: "Even though the team is successful, our focus is not just about winning. It's helping these kids play to the best of their ability. There is simply too much emphasis on winning and not enough emphasis on developing skills." Bob estimated that 80 percent of coaches at this level are drill-masters, not teachers. Teachers communicate an understanding of the game and can teach skills. Drill-masters just blow a whistle. They may know systems, but they don't teach fundamentals.

Blaine Stoughton, a former NHL all-star who also played in Europe, echoed what many coaches and players have said. There's way too much early focus on winning in minor hockey. There's too much structure, and too many games. Blaine said, "Think about it. In a game there's only one puck and you might get to handle the puck for a few seconds. In practice everyone can have a puck and you have plenty of opportunity to work with it to develop your skills. Which situation do you think is more likely to develop skills?" It's obvious.

I asked former NHL star Frank Mahovlich about developing the complete player. Frank said, "First, you need the physical ability. Then you need good coaching and competition to improve. Competition is important; however, kids play too many games."

Then Frank asked, "How come 11 of the top 20 scorers in the NHL today are Europeans?"[2] He answered himself: "It's because they have good coaching, and they emphasize skill development and practice. They practice all week long — even at the senior levels. It's the same in anything, from hockey to ballet: to become good you have to practice a lot more than you play or perform."

Practice can make perfect, or at least it can markedly improve a young player's skills, and, ultimately, the game. Too much of an emphasis on competition early on may come at the expense of quality practice time and skill development. Tiger Woods highlights

---

2 On March 28, 2001, a day after Frank and I spoke, NHL stats revealed that 10 of the top 15 scorers in the NHL were European.

the value of practice for developing the complete player. After winning his third Memorial golf tournament, Tiger said, "When I am at home I'd much rather practice than play. Even as a little boy I never liked playing when I was at home. I preferred practice. I love practicing. That's me."

Pat Quinn is a coach who has aided the development of many complete players. I asked Pat if he thought that there was too much of an early emphasis on winning. Pat's response was both a yes and a no. Yes, in that an early overemphasis on winning can come at the expense of developing kids' abilities. And no, in that the game is about winning. And early on, it's important for children to learn to compete, to win the puck, and win the little battles.

Ryan Walter, a former NHL player, now a TV broadcaster, is a hockey dad who is involved with minor hockey. For a couple of years Ryan ran a successful bantam hockey program that emphasized skills and values. Ryan believes in building an atmosphere through words, actions, and communication in which players are encouraged to grow, improve, and compete. Ryan said, "A great basketball coach who I respect said, 'I don't concern myself a lot with winning. I'm more concerned about practicing and executing the actions and attitudes that create the win.'" Ryan added, "Building hockey players and people has less instant gratification than a win but is much more satisfying to both parties."

Ryan believes that leadership is influence. Coaching at every level of hockey needs more leaders who mold, teach, and positively influence hockey skill and life development of their players. Ryan said, "Showing our players how to compete hard and create success within the scope of the rules will allow us all to develop more balanced leaders for society — and fewer criminals believing that breaking the rules is a normal part of the game."

Bobby Orr speaks passionately about the need for more emphasis on values in the game, especially at the youngest levels. Talking about six- to nine-year-olds, he says, "These are our children. They are the future. They're impressionable. They want to learn and to have fun." Bobby feels that too many coaches and parents put winning too far in front and put the kids in positions they are not ready to handle: "There's a problem. We're turning kids away from the game. We've got to let our kids go, have fun, and not over-structure them. The values we can teach them while they're having fun they can use for whatever career they choose. If we don't have parents and coaches buying in, we don't have a chance."

Harry Neale, a former NHL and WHA coach and general manager who is now a noted broadcaster, notes that smaller kids are being pushed out of hockey by the age of 13 because the game can be too physical for a slow developer. Harry points to little league football, which classifies players by size as well as age, as an example hockey might learn from.

Healthy people have a natural desire to excel. A coach can nurture that desire and a love of the game. Harry identifies love of the game as an important ingredient in a player's success and agrees that coaches can instill it in players. He said, "The first five coaches you have at the developmental stages can nurture that passion. The pro coach can only reinforce it."

Parents also have an impact on developing the complete player. Again, it's a matter of values. When I speak to groups of hockey coaches, one of the most difficult challenges the coaches describe at the developmental levels is dealing with parents. Understandably, parents want their children to excel. Too often it's at any price, and without consideration or respect for the team, for other players, for support people, or the game.

In addition to the reports cited earlier of hockey parents beating each other, I've been told many tales: of parents challenging coaches because the coach didn't do what the parent wanted, of parents abusing their child because he didn't do what he was supposed to do, and of parents threatening players on other teams or spectators in the stands because of what happened on the ice. All of this shapes a context for growing the complete player.

Recently, a parent told me that another father walked into his

12-year-old son's dressing room between periods and grabbed the boy and scolded him for being knocked down and not retaliating. Then he pushed the child hard against the wall and told him to "toughen up." When the coach tried to intervene the father grabbed the coach and threw him against the wall, and then stormed out of the kids' dressing room.

I recall Cliff Ronning and his dad telling me a story about Cliff's days in junior hockey. His dad said, "I was watching a game out of town and Cliff had scored a couple of goals and this guy sitting in front of me starts yelling, 'Kill number seven' [Cliff's number]. He's yelling, 'Kill him,' and all the while he's standing there with his six- or seven-year-old kid. And I say to him, 'That player you're saying to kill is my son. How would you feel if someone was yelling to kill your son?' And it didn't seem to faze him a bit."

Fan violence is inflammatory and frightening. It reflects our values and it can affect our game. Two years ago the brother of a goalie on a junior team I worked with died in a tragic boating accident. When the goalie went to play a rival team, a number of the fans started chanting the name of his deceased brother to upset him.

Some parents and fans get so emotionally aroused during a game that they react inappropriately and without realizing what they're doing. One way to help an overly emotional parent, "fan," or coach become more aware is to videotape their emotional game behavior, and then play it back to them later. In a quieter moment, some that I've known have been embarrassed and shocked back to sanity.

Last but not least, league officials can have a significant impact on stewarding the developmental context and values of the game of hockey. When the game is not played according to the rules, it becomes more difficult to expect players to maintain composure, exercise self-control, and not retaliate.

Hockey is one of the few sports where a player is allowed to contact an opposing player with his stick. That being the case, players must be held response-able for managing their sticks — and their emotions. Even if unintended, high-sticking injuries can occur and retaliation can lead to violence. Some years ago, I spoke with Brian

O'Neill, who was then an NHL vice president and director of hockey operations. A big part of his job was to act as the league's chief disciplinarian. I asked if something more might be done to control the use of the stick, such as no stick-checking above the waist. He told me that the league had made a concerted effort to reduce violence and stick-work and would continue to do so. There have been improvements, but there's still more to be done.

Shortly after the McSorley–Brashear incident, Scott Niedermeyer of the New Jersey Devils was suspended for 10 games for hitting an opposing player in the head with his stick in retaliation for a high elbow. When asked about the severity of his penalty, Niedermeyer said that if the league was trying to clean things up and attempting to get rid of the high elbows, high sticks, late hits, hits from behind, then he was all for it.

Paul Kariya, one of the NHL's more exciting players, was the recipient of a violent cross-check to the head that left him with a concussion and disabled for months. When I asked him about the violence in the game he said, "Hockey is a high-speed, intense, physical game. In the ebb and flow of the game, stuff happens." While Paul said that the overwhelming majority of players in the NHL have no intent to injure, he added, "One obvious solution to the violence is stiffer penalties. It would make for a better game."

Leagues could make some rule changes, especially in youth hockey. Some suggestions include no stick contact above the waist; less tolerance for high sticks, regardless of intention; no high elbows; no late hits; no fighting below junior ranks (and more control of fighting at the junior level); automatic suspension for a player who draws a flagrant penalty where intent to injure appears to be involved; and penalizing coaches who can't control their players (or bench). And officiating should be improved to make sure the rules are enforced properly — more training and better pay for referees, and, where possible, a two-referee system should be introduced.

While I was writing this chapter I attended a Junior A hockey game and was disappointed with the play and the officiating. Instead of fast, physical hockey, the players were hacking, holding, and punching each other all over the ice. The referee was unable to see it all or to make the calls. He lost control of the game, resulting in an escalation of the violence and a deterioration of the play.

Refereeing junior hockey is not an easy task. More experienced officials, and perhaps an extra referee, might have helped.

Finally, as we in North America are increasingly exposed to the international game, a number of hockey experts have suggested that the North American rink is just too small for the bigger, faster players and the trap style of defensive hockey that has become so prevalent. It has been suggested that a move to the larger, international-sized ice surface would lead to a faster game with less clutching and grabbing and goonery. I, for one, would enjoy seeing the world's best players playing on a bigger ice surface with more space and opportunity to showcase their skills. However, financial considerations within the North American professional leagues make that unlikely.

Rule changes, improved refereeing, and larger ice surfaces won't help if we don't also work to steward our values. A recent study on reducing violence in hockey[3] suggested that the solutions to the problem require commitment and action from everyone involved: the players, the coaches, the parents, the fans, and the officials. I agree. It's about all of us who enjoy hockey being more response-able to ensure a healthy balance of speed, skill, finesse, power, toughness, aggression, and control is maintained in this wonderful game.

---

3 For more information, see *Eliminating Violence in Hockey*, by Bernie Pascal, a report commissioned by British Columbia's minister of sport and the British Columbia Amateur Hockey Association, May 2000.

Index